Stained Glass

Beginner

Published by

krause publications
An F&W Publications Company

700 East State Street • Iola, WI 54990-0001
715-445-2214 • 888-457-2873
www.krause.com

Please call or write for our free catalog of publications.
Our toll-free number to place an order or obtain a free catalog is
(800) 258-0929.

Library of Congress Catalog Number: 2003108447
ISBN: 0-87349-683-3

Edited by Maria L. Turner
Designed by Gary Carle

Dedication

This book is dedicated to Linda, Mia, and Paige— my family. Thanks for keeping me on track.

Acknowledgments

I extend my deepest gratitude to my wife Linda Alfuth for the hours upon hours of photography and her patience in working day and night with me.

Thank you to Rick Bartkowiak, my lifelong friend, for convincing me to try stained glass art and to Leroy Newby for giving me the space to work and learn from a truly talented (but very reserved) artist.

Finally, thanks to the Krause Publications personnel who helped guide me and encourage me to get this book done: Maria Turner, Julie Stephani, Sarah Werbelow, Paul Kennedy, Marilyn McGrane, Jamie Griffin, and Don Gulbrandsen.

Contents

Introduction

You have just purchased the most comprehensive stained glass beginner book on the market. When you complete this book, you will have the fundamental skills for working in stained glass. You will learn skills you can apply to any flat surface or three-dimensional glass project that your imagination can create.

This book is designed as a reference book, allowing you to easily go back and review sections you may have difficulty with. However, it is recommended that you complete each section before moving on, as each section builds from the previous one.

We will start with a brief introduction of what is involved and what to expect as you venture through this book. Within each section, there are detailed instructions with numerous pictures displaying examples. Included in the back of the book are a variety of designs and patterns used in creating several lamps and a master pattern, which may be used to create your own designs.

Please note that the beautiful chapter opener photographs showcase pieces that are not covered in this book. These stained glass projects are meant more as inspirational "gallery" pieces to show you what you can create if you stick with it and move beyond the basics covered here.

This book includes everything you need to develop your stained glass artist from within, so enjoy!

Getting Started

When starting in the art of stained glass, there are some basics every beginner needs to get acquainted with. They are covered in this section.

Lead Came vs. Copper Foil

You could say "copper foil" and "lead came" are the skeletal frame, which when combined with solder and glass, bring your stained glass project all together.

Lead Came

Lead came is mainly used in the construction of windows and/or very large projects. This bendable material is made of lead and comes in 6-foot lengths, several widths, and various shapes. The lead is cut to the proper length and then bent and shaped around your piece of glass. As you can see in the photo here, the glass fits easily in the ready-made channel.

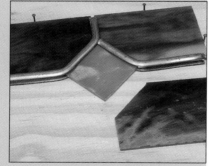

Joined together by soldering at each connecting point.

The use of lead came provides additional strength and stability when creating very large pieces, such as church windows.

Working with lead came requires additional tools and instructions, which will not be covered in this book. It requires a completely different approach during the construction part of your project. I wanted this book to focus solely on the copper foil method, as that seems to be the best for beginners.

Copper Foil

The use of copper foil (a technique you will learn in this book) is used mainly in lamp-making and for window hangings or other small projects. Originally, copper foil came in thin sheets of "copper," which were no thicker than a piece of paper.

Unlike in the past, this sheet comes with a tape backing, which helps keep the foil in place.

Based on the thickness of the glass you are working on, you can use a paper cutter to cut the copper foil to the proper width.

A paper cutter makes it easy to get accurate cuts for the width needed.

These narrow strips of copper foil are then crimped around the edges of your glass pieces.

Copper foil partially crimped around a piece of glass.

Applying copper foil gives you the necessary means to solder two pieces of glass together.

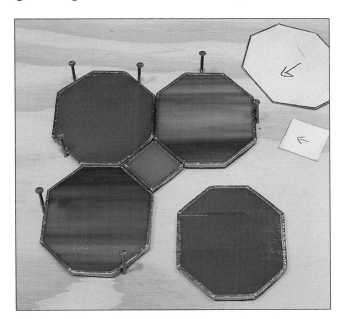

Group of pieces foiled and almost ready to be soldered.

Today, there is "copper foil tape," which makes the job of foiling much easier.

Foil with backing pulled away and ready to be attached to glass.

Since one side is sticky (like tape), it easily adheres to the glass edge, keeping it in place as you foil. Copper foil tape comes in a variety of widths and thicknesses. As you can imagine, the introduction of copper foil tape in 1980 was a welcome change to the difficulty of working with the often-slippery copper foil.

If there is a negative side to foil tape, the only problem I have encountered is that the glue used on the backside of the tape will ooze out from the heat of the soldering iron. This oozing melted-glue backing causes a sticky, gooey mess on your glass, making it difficult – but not impossible – to clean. It's a small price to pay, however, for the convenience of using foil with tape backing.

Selecting Color and Design

In working with stained glass, you will find that choosing a few tasteful colors usually results in a better-finished piece than when using a variety of colors. If blending colors is not your strong point, take advantage of a color wheel to guide you. Color wheels are available at any art supply store.

Color Wheel

The color wheel is a great tool to use to help you with your color choices. Basically, it consists of the primary, secondary, and tertiary colors. A number of different combinations of these are possible.

Cool colors:
Blues, violets, and greens.

Warm colors:
Reds, yellows, and oranges.

Complementary colors:
Colors opposite each other on the color wheel; for example, red and green.

Analogous colors:
Colors next to each other on the color wheel. They have a color in common. For example: red, red orange, and red violet.

Triad colors:
Three colors equal distance apart on the wheel; for example, green, orange, and blue.

Split complementary colors:
Three colors of any hue and the two adjacent to the complementary; for example, red, yellow-green, and blue-green.

Monochromatic colors:
One color plus its tints and shades. Colors are used to express a mood. For example, cool colors give a calming effect, whereas the warm colors indicate excitement or happiness.

Also, take notice of the simple designs used; you don't really need a difficult pattern to turn out a great- looking project.

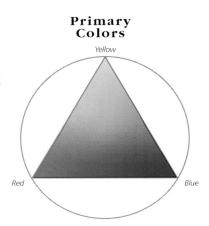

Primary Colors

Yellow

Red

Blue

I have included some patterns at the back of the book (pages 117-123) that were designed not only to

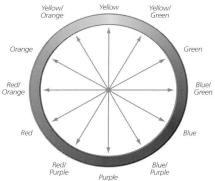

Complementary Colors

Yellow/Orange — Yellow — Yellow/Green

Orange — Green

Red/Orange — Blue/Green

Red — Blue

Red/Purple — Blue/Purple

Purple

achieve a beautiful end result, but also with the beginner in mind.

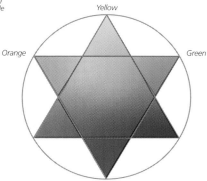

Secondary Colors

Yellow

Orange — Green

Purple

These pictures show how you can take a simple design, using just two colors, and make several beautiful lamp variations.

Glass

Glass is made primarily from silica sand, limestone, and soda ash. The three are mixed together, put into a glass furnace, and heated to about 3,000 degrees, at which point, the ingredients melt into a liquid that can be made into sheets.

Adding in different metal oxides during melting results in colored glass. Selenium or gold additives create red, yellow, and pink glass, while cobalt is added for blue, and sulfur makes a brownish tint. The oxide used has a significant bearing on the final cost of glass. Since selenium and gold are expensive, glass in red, yellow, orange, and pink will also be more costly to buy.

Here, you can see my hand, behind the glass, which is an example of cathedral glass.

Basic Types

There are several variations of glass available, yet they can be broken down into two basic types: opalescent and cathedral.

Opalescent glass, while not transmitting as much light, will give a warm glow to the finished piece.

Cathedral glass, being more transparent, will allow a lot of light through, displaying bright colors.

I prefer to use the opalescent glass more often in lamps. It tends to hide the bulb behind the glass, evenly dispersing the light. I prefer cathedral (or a combination of both) in windows or pieces that will be displayed in direct sunlight or where the source of light is further away.

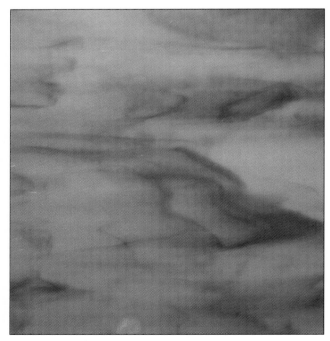

You can't see it, but my hand is also behind this piece of glass, which illustrates the qualities of opalescent glass.

Surface Textures

"Stained glass" is not always manufactured with the same smooth surface as clear glass. It may come in various textures.

The use of textured glass adds yet another dimension to how your project will look when completed.

Working with textured glass can be difficult. Scoring can be a challenge; the wheel of the cutter will follow grooves in the glass, making it difficult to follow

One textured glass, called "ripple," is smooth on one side, still making it easy to score and grind, but slightly difficult to foil.

Other types of textured glass include: crackle, glue chip, granite, hammered, reamy, and seedy. They all have their own unique texture and therefore present slight differences in how they are scored, ground, and foiled.

A good example of a piece of glass with rough surface, above.

Ripple glass.

your pattern. Copper foiling a textured piece also can be rough on your hands when flattening out the foil on the edges.

A smooth surface is usually easier to foil, grind, and score than a rough surface; however, the hardness of the glass also plays a key factor in ease of scoring.

With practice, you will develop the skill of working with various surfaces and will find the rewards of the added interest that textured glass can offer.

Tools Needed

Working with stained glass requires the use of the following tools:

- pliers
- glasscutter
- glass grinder
- solder
- soldering iron
- small water bottle
- stickpins
- scissors
- masking tape
- flux brush (able to withstand oily substances without losing its bristles)
- carbon, tracing, and regular papers
- flux
- safety glasses

Detailed descriptions and where to find all the necessary tools are located in Section 2, beginning on page 18.

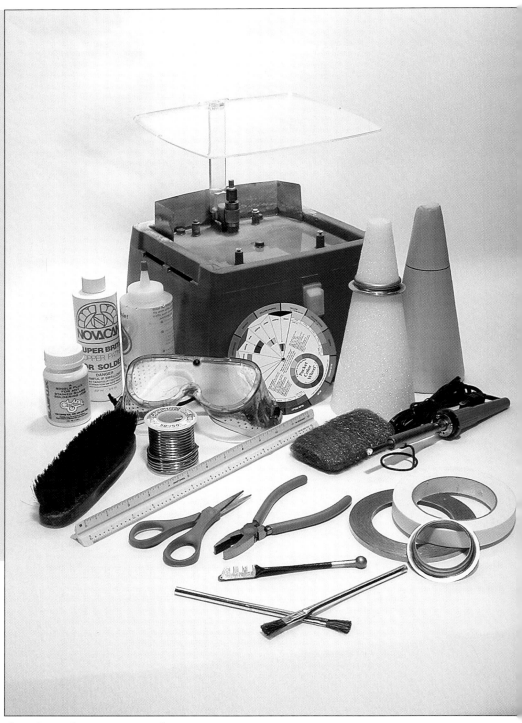

A variety of necessary tools.

Workspace

You will be more efficient with the tools you need close at hand.

Design your work area around safety. Following these simple rules will help provide a safe and enjoyable environment to work in.

More often than not, you are dealing with sharp edges, especially once the glass is cut. Use extra care while handling the pieces until they reach the grinding stage.

If you have the available workspace, it's nice to have designated areas for each step required. For example, have a grinding area. At times, water sprays from the grinding wheel, getting your work area wet. Or when soldering, you will get flux on the surface of your workspace. This can be very difficult to clean off, leaving behind an oily area to work in.

If you do not have the advantage of a large work area, by using both sides of your board (which you use as your work surface), you can designate one side for grinding and soldering, and the other for cutting. Utilizing both sides allows you to maintain one surface that is always clear of flux or water.

Keeping It Clean

There will always be small pieces of glass that chip off while grinding or removing excess glass, which is a good reason to always wear safety glasses when performing either of these steps.

Always keep your workspace clean and clear of glass scraps by using your brush frequently. Small pieces of glass stick to your clothes and shoes and end up being carried wherever you go. On occasion, I use a shop vacuum to do a really thorough cleaning, especially after I have done a lot of cutting or grinding.

Soldering Iron Cautions

The soldering iron is another safety consideration in your workspace. To avoid a fire, never leave your iron unattended while it is on. Fortunately, these irons are well-designed with an adequate handle, helping you to avoid serious burns. When plugging the iron into an outlet, make sure the cord is not draped near your feet, so you won't accidentally pull the iron off the table when leaving your work area.

Fire and burns are not the only considerations when using your soldering iron. The fumes created from melting solder are poisonous. That's why it is imperative to use a fan when soldering to move the fumes away from you. Besides a fan, make sure there is plenty of ventilation where you solder.

Improper handling of solder itself can also be dangerous. Solder is made from a combination of lead and tin, with lead being the poisonous material. After working with solder, make sure to wash your hands thoroughly.

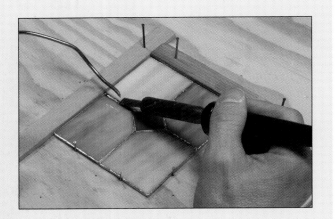

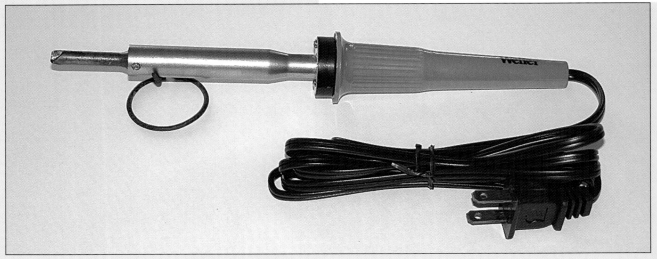

Solder irons, like the ones shown in the photos above, are designed today with safety in mind; however, it's never a bad idea to use caution when learning how to handle your iron..

This section provides a detailed list of supplies you will need to get started in stained glass, along with suggestions on where to find them.

Common Supplies

The items in this section are those used for more than just stained glass-making. These are simple items that you may already have on hand, but will want to move to your work area so they are readily available as you create your pieces.

Adhesive Bandages

As one might expect, working with glass can result in a cut or nick to a finger or hand every now and again. I like to have a box of bandages on hand that contains a lot of small bandages. Yes, expect to have a few small cuts once and awhile. If you are able to get by without any of these minor "battle wounds," consider yourself lucky.

Bench Brush

A fine-bristled brush is essential for removing the glass scraps from your work area. You will want a brush with fine bristles, since that type works better for removal of the very small pieces of glass.

Any good brush will do for use as a bench brush.

Carbon Paper

Carbon paper is used in transferring the original pattern from the tracing paper onto your pattern paper. You won't need to buy a lot of carbon paper, one or two sheets should last you for a long time.

Masking Tape

In lamp-making, masking tape acts as a drawing surface, used for adding your reference lines.

Polystyrene form covered in masking tape and ready for reference lines.

After numerous lamps, the tape will become unusable from the flux and solder residue. By just reapplying new tape, you can start with a clean surface. You will only need to purchase one roll of tape to start. Each form does not require much tape to cover it entirely.

Nails

Nails of ¾" to 1" lengths are used to keep pieces in place while soldering.

Paper

For making patterns, purchase a heavier weight plain white paper, preferably a cardstock type.

Plywood Board

A piece of plywood makes for a sound work surface. I recommend an approximate size of 2-foot x 4-foot x ¾" piece of plywood or larger, but choose whatever works best in your work area. Keep in mind, though, that a piece of at least ¾" thickness will lay flatter and is less likely to warp.

Rubber Gloves

Rubber gloves are necessary when adding a patina (copper plating).

Ruler

You will want at least a 12" ruler.

Scissors

Scissors are used for cutting out your paper patterns.

Small Cleaning Brush

A small brush, approximately 1" x 3" with ¾" bristles, is used to scrub your project clean before applying the finish.

This plywood piece is about 2-foot x 4-foot x ¾".

Polystyrene Form

Forms of various dimensions can be found at most craft stores. The form used in this book has a height of 9" with a base diameter of approximately 3¾". You will only need to purchase one form. It can be used again and again.

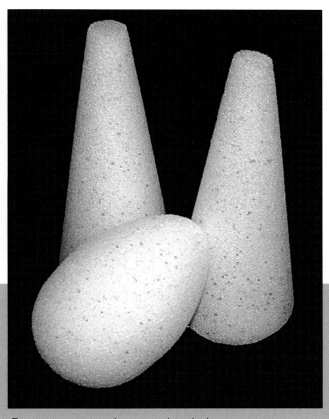

Forms can come in several varieties, even egg-shaped.

Small Water Bottle

Water is necessary to prevent the glass from breaking when heat is generated during grinding. All grinders have a reservoir to hold water and usually come with a small sponge, which is located behind the grinding wheel. Kept wet, this sponge will keep your glass cool.

While grinding, water has a tendency to spray out around the grinding wheel, depleting your supply a little at a time. This is when it's convenient to have a water bottle around for an additional supply. Most grinders have the option of attaching

Small-diameter wheel mounted on top.

Stickpins

Stickpins are needed for holding your glass pieces in place when working on a polystyrene form (primarily in lamp-making) prior to spot soldering it together. If you plan on making lamps, plan to get a box of 50 pins to start.

Typical style grinder, with water bottle.

an additional (smaller diameter) grinding wheel on the top. This addition is usually beyond the water supply sponge, making it necessary to add water manually.

Pieces in place and ready to be spot soldered.

Tracing Paper

Use tracing paper when tracing the patterns from the back of this book or original patterns you create. Making patterns in this way will allow you to preserve the original pattern template.

Wood Strips

Get two or three scrap pieces of wood, approximately 1" wide x ¼" to ½" thick and about a 1-foot long. These strips will be used when working on flat panel projects to help hold your pieces in place.

General Supplies

This section includes those items that you likely do not have already, but can readily find at a local hardware store.

Clear Glass

Start with a piece of clear glass that is 1-square-foot in size, at least when practicing. You will want to practice, so you may even want to pick up a little more than 1 foot and you may want to consider finding used glass.

A good source of used glass can be found at your local junk dealer (that is, if you can still find one). You can pick up an old window that is relatively inexpensive to practice on. Try to find one that you can remove the glass from the frame easily.

Clear glass doesn't have the added materials used in making stained glass, leaving it much smoother. This smooth surface helps make clear glass easier to score and break. All you need is one quick score line followed by a little pressure at one end, and the pieces separate. With stained glass, sometimes it just doesn't work that smoothly.

Flux

An oily fluid used in soldering, flux helps the flow of solder onto the copper foil thereby providing a smoother, more even application. One bottle of flux will last a long time.

Flux Brush

Although any good small brush will work, specific "flux" brushes are made to last longer in oily substances. They are usually about ½" wide. One brush is plenty to start with.

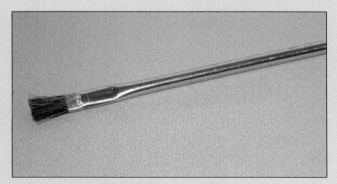

This brush is made for flux.

Glasscutter

Choices are usually limited when buying a glasscutter at a hardware store, but I still prefer the standard glasscutters to anything more specialized.

One such standard cutter is 01-122 Gold Tip Ball End, 130 degrees or 114 degrees.

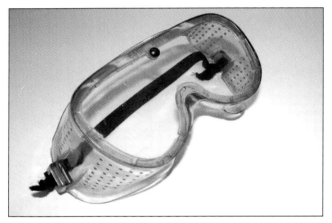

A Carbide Fletcher Glasscutter is one typical brand.

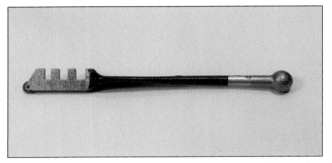

Purchase any good safety glasses that cover your eyes well.

Safety Glasses

Safety glasses are strongly recommended while cutting or breaking glass. They are also needed if a face shield is not supplied with your grinder.

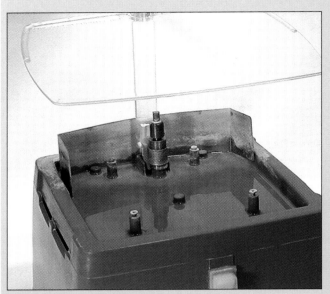

While grinding, always use your grinder shield, which is usually standard equipment with a grinder.

Solder

Solder is a mixture of tin-lead alloys and the numbers used to identify solder refer to the percentage mix of tin and lead. The first number is always the tin. If there is more tin alloy, there will be less heat needed to melt the solder.

For stained glass work, use "50/50" solder. One pound will be sufficient to start with. This is 50 percent lead mixed with 50 percent tin. (Other appropriate ranges are 60/40 and 63/37.)

Canfield 50/50 solder.

Soldering Iron

Look for a "soldering iron" instead of a "soldering gun" because the gun gets too hot for working in stained glass and when the glass gets too hot, it will break. I recommend an 80-watt iron with a ¼"-wide tip.

At first, the ¼"-wide tip may seem a little too wide, but once you get better at soldering, you will appreciate the wider tip as it maintains heat longer and more evenly.

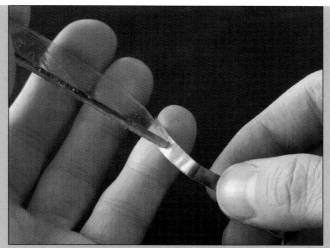

When choosing the width of copper foil, be sure there is slight overhang on each side of the glass.

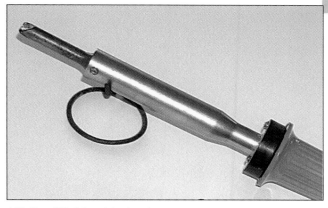

Weller SP-80 soldering iron.

Steel Wool

Used for wiping the tip of your soldering iron to keep it clean, any "fine 0" grade steel wool will work well.

Specialty Items

The items contained within this section are those that can be found at any stained glass supply store or at the retailers listed in the Resources, page 124.

Copper Foil

Copper foil comes in a variety of thicknesses and widths. Determine the width of tape you will need based on the thickness of your glass. You will want to have approximately ¹⁄₆₄" overhang on each side of the glass.

Deciding which "thickness" of tape you need is a personal decision, but here are a few things to consider.

Disadvantages of thicker tape: It will add additional space between your glass pieces, which will slightly change the overall dimension of your project. Eventually, space is created between pieces and you will either have to compensate by grinding more or adding additional solder to fill in the gaps.

Thicker tape also can be more difficult to crimp than thinner foil, making it a little harder on your hands.

Advantages of thicker tape: It is more durable and won't break as easily while foiling.

If you work carefully, thinner tape has a tendency to lay flatter allowing the soldering iron to glide easier on top of a flatter foiled surface. Thinner tape also crimps easier.

Foil comes in various widths (5/32", 3/16", 7/32", 1/4", and 3/8") and thickness (1mm, 1.25mm, and 1.5mm). I recommend starting out with one roll each of 7/32" and 3/16" wide, both with a thickness of 1.25mm.

Glass Diamond Grinder

There are many grinders on the market. I have used the same grinder now for more than 30 years—a Glastar Model G3—and it still works great.

As a beginner, you won't need the biggest or the most expensive grinder you can find. Start off with an inexpensive grinder (less than $100). You can always move up to a larger, more powerful one later if you feel the need. Most grinders come with a 3/4" wheel, which I find to be more than adequate for most projects.

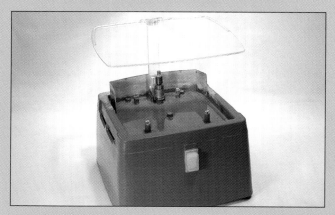

Shown with the table removed, allowing a better angle on your glass.

As you see by the picture, I have added an additional smaller-diameter wheel to the top of my original grinder wheel. This comes in very handy when working on very tight, inside curves. A second wheel is definitely not a necessity for the beginner, but as you become more experienced, you will find that it can be useful.

Lamp Base

As you can see by the examples, there are many different shapes, styles, and sizes of lamp bases. I have found bases at antique stores, garage sales, auctions, or lamp suppliers, some of which are found in the Resources, page 124.

Typical new lamp bases available today.

Lamp ring

A lamp ring is a brass ring that you attach to the top of your lamp to connect it to a lamp base. These come in different diameters, but the most common size for lamps is 2¼".

Two standard-diameter lamp rings.

Patina

Copper or black patina is made for solder. Make sure you select the correct type of patina for your application. Some patinas only work on solder, others only on lead. The product packaging specifies which will work for each surface. Follow the manufacturers instructions and use a brush or soft rag to apply the patina until you reach the desired color.

Pliers

Get a good-quality pair of pliers. You should look for a good squared-off front on the jaws, since you will use the jaws occasionally to nip off very small pieces of scrap.

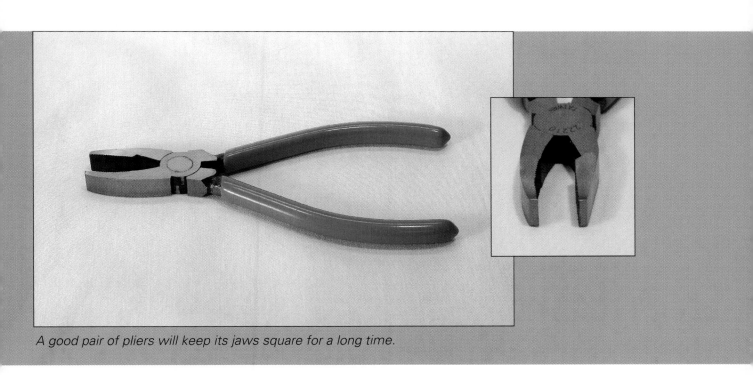

A good pair of pliers will keep its jaws square for a long time.

Stained Glass

When stocking your glass supply, figure that you will need approximately 1 square-foot of glass for each color used in a typical small lamp. With flat-panel projects, the amount of glass needed is based on how many colors used and the overall finished size of your project. You can safely figure the total amount of glass needed by multiplying the finished size by one-and-half times. It's always a good idea to get more than you need.

Not all pieces will come out on the first try. On difficult patterns, you may find yourself making several attempts before you learn how your glass breaks on a score line. You will find glass from some manufacturers will follow a score line better than others.

You may also need to make repairs on a previous project. If so, you will have the same glass on hand. Glass suppliers will usually cut any amount needed. Unlike clear glass, stained glass is mostly manufactured with one side smoother than the other, making one side easier to score.

Sometimes, the texture on the two sides is very difficult to distinguish. By closely inspecting the glass, however, you should be able to determine which side is smoother. When scoring glass, you will want to use the smoother side.

An adequate supply of glass for the hobbyist.

Your glasscutter is a versatile tool that is used a great deal in creating stained glass art. In this section, not only are proper grip and glasscutter maintenance tips covered, but more importantly, various techniques are explained with practice exercises detailed.

Clean Work Area

Before you get started, sweep your work surface clean. If any dirt, glass chips, or debris of any kind is under your glass while scoring, the glass could break unexpectedly. Also avoid any irregularities in your work surface like warped wood or gouges in the wood. You need a clean, smooth surface to adequately score glass on.

Working with Patterns

Begin by creating some patterns to practice on. You can use the patterns included here or you can make up a few of your own. If you make your own, be sure to keep them simple.

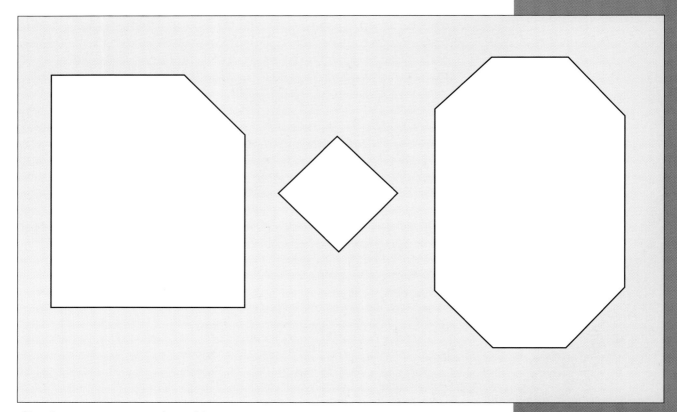

Simple patterns to practice with.

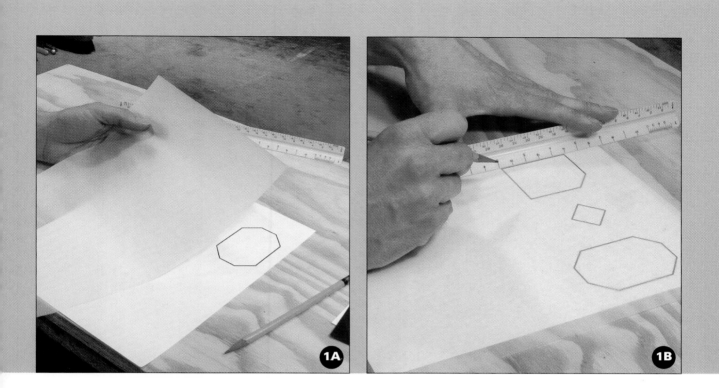

The following steps will guide you in using the sample patterns:

1. *Trace the patterns onto tracing paper, as shown above. Use a ruler whenever possible, especially when tracing straight lines.*

2. *After the patterns are traced onto the tracing paper, transfer them onto the pattern paper using carbon paper, as shown below.*

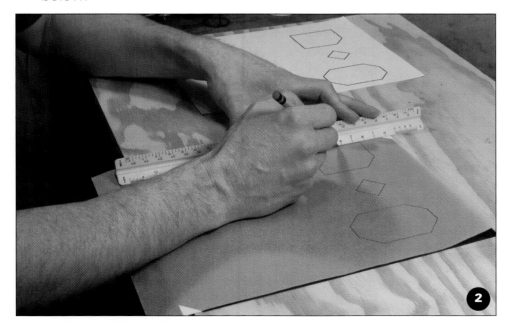

3. *Cut patterns out with your scissors, keeping as close to the pattern lines as possible. Notice in the photo at right the addition of arrows to depict the direction of the grain on the glass.*

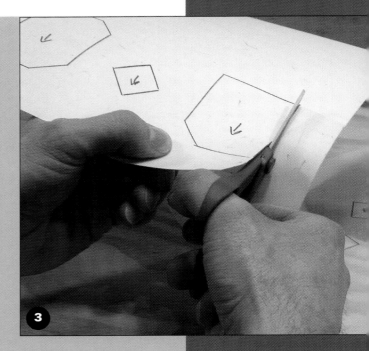

Grain in glass is created when the glass is rolled out during manufacturing. Grain can appear as either actual grooves in the glass or as a color pattern in the glass, all going in the same direction.

When you have glass that has a distinct grain, always determine the direction you would like it to go on your paper patterns, prior to cutting your glass pieces out. You may want to experiment with the grain by having each individual color go its own direction, i.e. all red pieces going one direction, and all blues going another. Your finished project will have a better look when the grain of each color you use is going in the same direction.

Proper Grip

How you hold your glasscutter is essential in developing a good technique, allowing you more control, comfort, and ease of use. As you can see in the photograph, the classic style glasscutter has a rest or saddle on both sides, made for your finger to rest on.

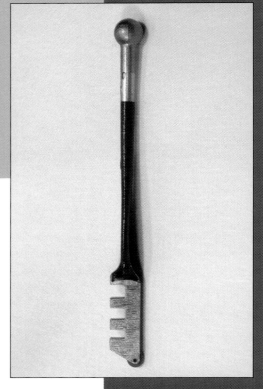

A standard Fletcher glasscutter.

The "rest" is where the downward pressure from your hand will be directly transferred.

The proper grip is obtained by first placing the cutter in your hand with the notches facing away from you and pinching the cutter between your thumb and middle finger, as shown.

Rest the neck of the cutter between your index and middle finger. When cutting glass, do not allow the neck of the cutter to apply any pressure between your fingers; it should simply rest in this position. Place your index finger in the saddle.

Initial grip of the cutter.

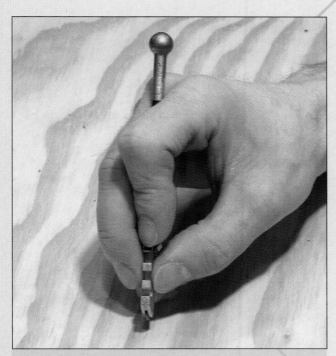

Allow the cutter to rest between your fingers.

Getting familiar with the proper grip may take some time to feel comfortable, so be patient. Take time to practice developing the proper grip right from the beginning and you will experience fewer difficulties when scoring your glass later.

Scoring

When it comes to "scoring," not all glass is created equal. The amount of pressure needed to make a good score will vary with the hardness of the glass you are working with. Scoring involves cutting slightly into the surface, creating a path for the break to follow. Never score on the same line more than once, as such a measure tends to dull your cutter prematurely.

Guiding your glasscutter around your pattern is controlled mainly with your wrist.

The accompanying photographs show two possible ways to position yourself while scoring glass: standing and sitting.

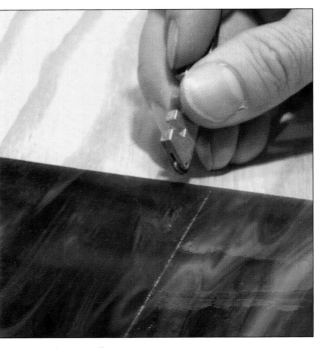

An actual score line.

Standing position: *Use your upper body (shoulder and arm) to help apply the downward pressure to your cutter.*

Sitting position: *While more comfortable, this method can be more difficult for mustering the adequate downward pressure needed.*

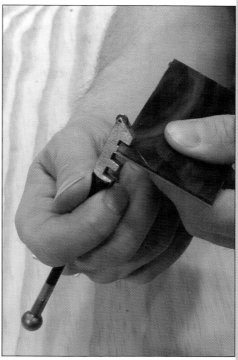

Use the notches of your glasscutter to remove unwanted glass, as shown in the two photos above.

The notches on the cutter provide a good way for breaking away unwanted glass, by grabbing onto the edge of the glass and then pulling down.

This book utilizes the push method of scoring, but the basic concept throughout this section can be applied to either method. You may want to experiment with both methods, just to see which is more comfortable for you. (Either method applies regardless of whether you are right- or left-handed.)

With the push method, I have found I can guide my cutter more accurately while giving me a better view of my pattern. I like to see where I'm going, as opposed to where I have been. It is also more convenient when working with very small patterns.

As you score glass, you will hear a distinct crackling sound. As time goes on, you will become familiar with this sound, which helps in determining how much pressure you will need to make a proper score line. As you will experience, scoring can take a lot of practice. If the score is too light, your glass may not break where you want it. When there is too much pressure, you can actually break the glass while scoring, and the break may not follow your score line.

In terms of the actual scoring procedure, there are two common practices used: push and pull.

One option is to pull the cutter towards you, as shown above, having the notches facing down.

For the push method, move the cutter away from you, with the notches facing up, as shown above.

Practice Exercises

Caution: *After cutting your pieces out, they will have very sharp edges!*

The following exercises will help you in developing the proper grip, the amount of pressure needed for scoring, and how the cutter reacts on glass.

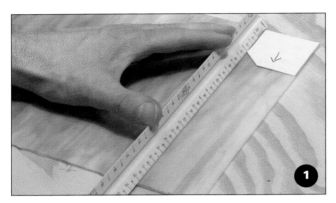

Pattern lined up on the first corner.

Pattern lined up on opposite side.

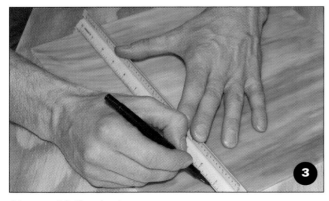

Your guideline is drawn.

Lesson 1: Reducing Glass to a Manageable Size

Reducing a large piece of glass to a more manageable size makes it safer to work with, helps minimize waste and reduces the overall amount of glass needed for a project.

In this first exercise, use clear glass, which is ideal to practice on. Clear glass is easy to score and remove unwanted glass from. I will be using stained glass, which will make it easier for me during my demonstrations since the patterns will show up better and the score lines are also easier for you to see.

Here, you will be making several practice pieces of each pattern, beginning with a piece of glass approximately 1-square-foot.

1. *Using one of the paper pattern pieces you created in the Working with Patterns section, page 28, place the pattern on one end of the glass, lining it up on the edge and placing the ruler just above it, as shown.*

2. *Firmly holding the ruler down, move the pattern to the other end of the glass piece and adjust your ruler so it is evenly lined up with the new pattern position, as shown.*

3. *Without moving the ruler, move the pattern out of the way, giving you room to draw a line across the entire length.*

Having a right-angled pattern, like a square or rectangle, allows you to line the pattern piece up with the edge of glass thereby enabling you to reduce your glass close to the actual size with little to no waste. If you can't easily line up a pattern on the edge, as with a triangle or other design, draw your reference line approximately ¼" away from the actual pattern piece edge, allowing the extra room needed for scoring. This adjustment process will be covered in more depth in the Projects sections.

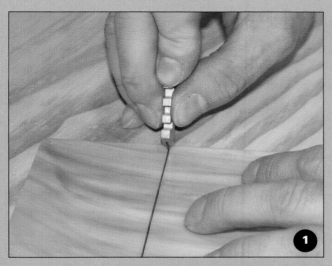

Start your score at the beginning of the line.

Steady, constant motion.

Lesson 2:
The "Score"

1. *Using a proper grip on your glasscutter, start your score by first lining up your cutter at the edge of the glass (closest to you) on the drawn guideline, as shown above.*

2. *Applying a steady downward pressure, move your cutter along the guideline, as shown above right.*

Be careful as you approach the end of the glass, as you should stop as close to the edge as possible, without running off of it. If you do run off the edge, you risk chipping the edge of the glass.

After you have completed the score line, you need to separate the pieces. With a piece of glass the size suggested (1-square-foot), there are several options you can use for separating.

Method 1

This is the method I most commonly use. It seems to work well with any size glass and straight score lines.

1. *Bring the glass close to the edge of your worktable, lining up the score line with the table's edge, as shown below.*

2. *Lightly holding the back edge of glass, raise the glass about ½" above the table.*

3. *Carefully, make a quick snap downward, separating the two pieces.*

Getting ready to separate in two.

Glass edge about a ½" above the table.

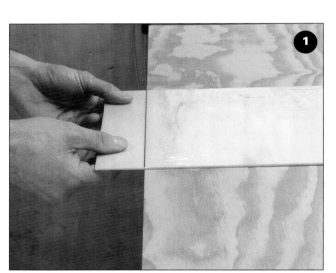

Glass lined up to the edge of the workbench.

One smooth downward motion, two pieces.

Method 2

This option works well with straight lines and larger pieces of glass.

1. *Place your cutter on your work surface, as shown below.*

2. *Position your glass on top of the "ball" end of the cutter, directly over the score line (approximately ½" from the edge), as shown at right.*

3. *Lightly apply pressure evenly to both sides of the glass until it breaks, as shown bottom right.*

Score line directly above the cutter.

With ball end of cutter away from you, place cutter on work surface.

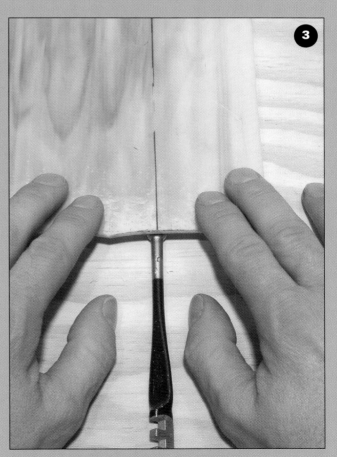

Pressure evenly applied to both sides.

Method 3

This method is by far the most dangerous of the three methods. It again involves using the ball end of the cutter, but in a different way. The danger comes from the likelihood of falling glass. When using this method, use extreme caution and only do this directly above your work surface, so if the glass does break, it won't have far to fall.

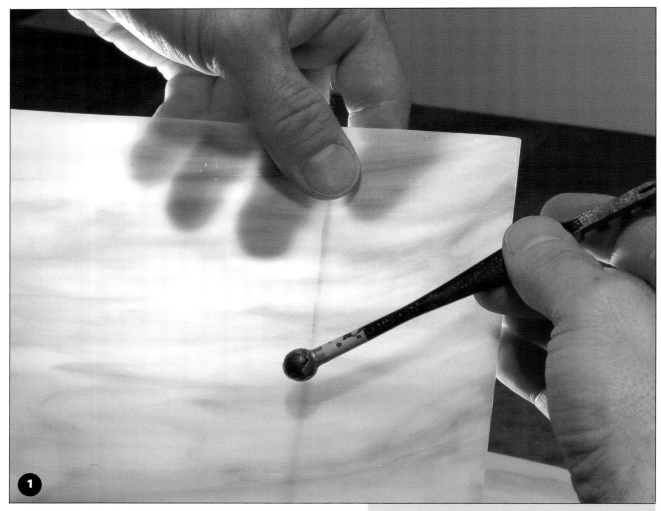

Light source from behind aids in seeing the score line.

1. *Hold the glass up to a light source with the scored side facing the light. With a light behind the glass, you should be able to clearly see the score line and/or the line you drew with the marker.*

Caution with Method 3:
If a piece of glass is falling, let it go! It is much safer to cut another piece than to try to catch it and risk serious injury.

Hold the cutter by the notch end. Using the ball end, lightly tap the glass directly along the score line. Continue moving slowly along the line, tapping lightly. You will actually see and hear the glass breaking as you go. The objective is not to tap too hard or to tap until the glass actually separates, but to help the glass break gradually along the score line.

2. After tapping from one end to the other along the score line, get a good grip on both edges of the glass with the score line in between and roll your wrists as if to bend the glass.

3. If all goes well, you should end up with a piece in each hand. If not, you may need to tap a little more.

Carefully hold the glass on both sides.

With some glass, the first two methods may not always work very well, since all glass is not made the same. Some glass follows a score line better than others, and some glass needs a little help to guide it along the score line. Since you can't tell by just looking at the glass, I would try all the methods in order, until you find the one that works best with your particular piece of glass.

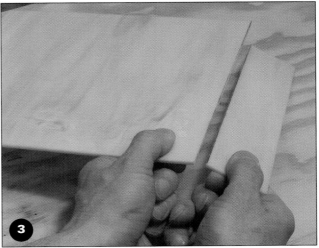

The scoring process is not as difficult as it may initially seem.

Lesson 3:
Working With Patterns

Now that you have reduced your larger piece of glass to a safer, more manageable size, the following steps will guide you through cutting out your patterns.

1. *Line up one of your pattern pieces on the edge of the glass, as shown at right. The nice thing about straight-edged patterns is that by lining them up on the edge, you can save yourself one or more cuts.*

2. *With your cutter in hand, hold your pattern down firmly with the other hand, making sure it doesn't move, and then line the cutter wheel up on the edge of your pattern, as shown at right.*

3. *Applying downward pressure, slowly guide your cutter along the outer edge of the pattern, as shown at right, striving not to stop unless you need to reposition yourself or the pattern. If you have to stop in the middle of a pattern to make an adjustment, start right where you left off. Avoid scoring on the same line more than once, as this practice will quickly dull your cutting wheel.*

The better you develop your scoring ability, the less waste you will have, the more accurate your pieces will fit, and the less grinding you will need in the end.

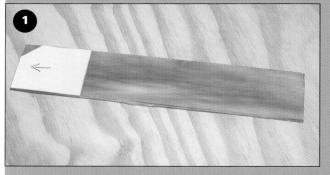

First pattern ready to score.

Cutter lined up on pattern's edge.

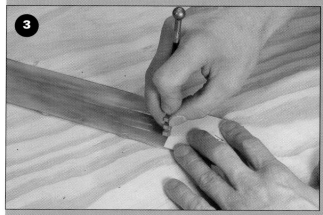

Steady motion, following the pattern.

Lesson 4: Removing Scrap From Cut Piece

Although the patterns are very simple, you still may need to remove excess glass from the original cutout. Breaking away excess glass can be tricky and a little difficult at times, based on the complexity of your pattern. It's not uncommon to have pieces break in the wrong place while removing waste from the glass. You may have to make several attempts to complete a difficult pattern.

Method 1: Using Cutter Teeth

This method works best when removing small pieces of glass from your pattern.

1. *Begin by holding the cutter in one of the two ways shown in the accompanying photos below.*

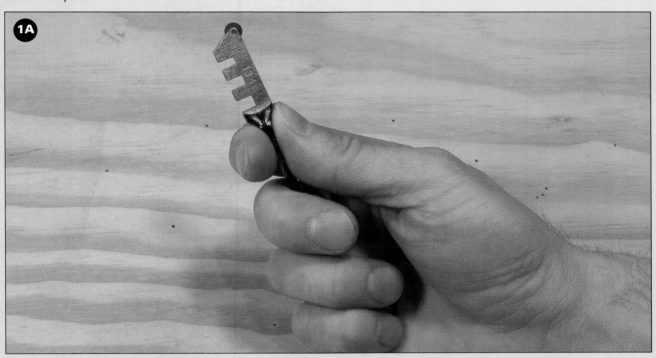

Two different ways to hold your cutter when using the teeth to remove glass.

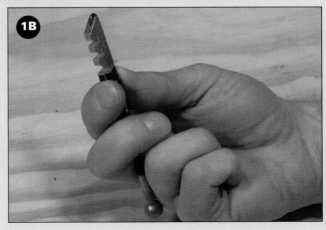

2. *The gaps between the teeth vary in width. Find the width that best fits your glass thickness. You want it to fit somewhat snugly, but not tight. Position the cutter on one end of the score line, as shown in the accompanying photos on this page.*

3. *Try to position the bottom edge of the tooth directly under the score line and with a firm grip on the glass, snap the cutter in a downward motion. The piece should break off following the score line.*

Keep in mind that this method will take practice, and it also may take some time to develop the proper motion.

Make sure you have a snug fit, not tight.

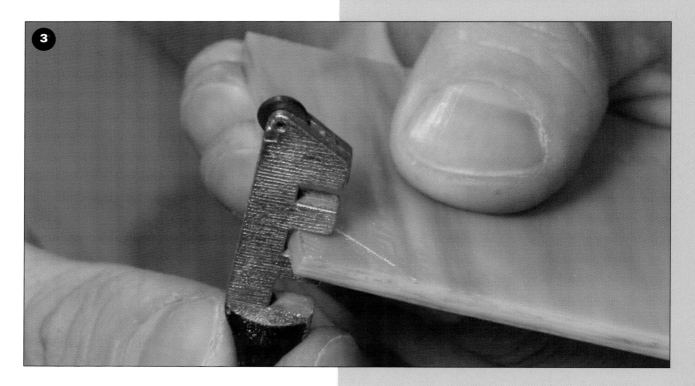

Method 2: Using Pliers

1. *Referring to the photo at right, position your pliers as close to the score line as possible, but do not go past it.*

2. *Where you start depends on how complex your pattern is, but since the practice patterns are not that complex, you can start on any edge. With one hand firmly gripping the glass and the other on your pliers, snap downward, as shown below, pulling the excess glass away.*

3. *Continue with step 2 around the piece, until all excess glass is removed. If you can't cleanly remove all the glass or you have small pieces remaining on the edge, they can be removed during the grinding stage.*

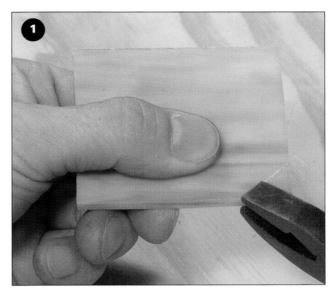

Pliers lined up close to the score line.

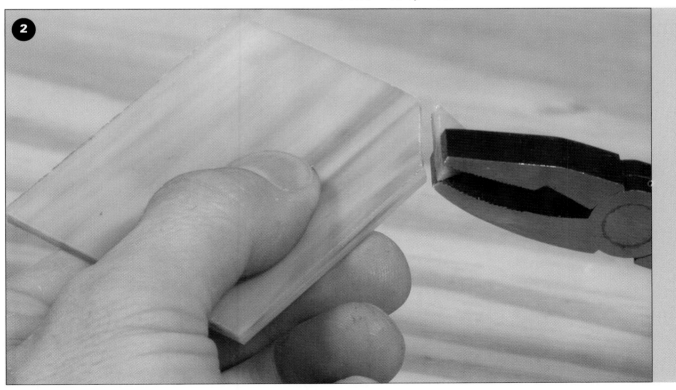

Snap downward with the hopes of obtaining a clean break, like the one shown here.

Method 3: Working on Curves

As this is a beginner's book, we will work mainly with simple patterns to make sure we get the basic fundamentals correct before moving on to more complex designs. Still, a brief overview of cutting curves may come in handy as you progress beyond the simplest designs.

The following examples demonstrate how to remove excess glass from a pattern with an inside curve. You can use your pliers or the glasscutter's "notches" to remove excess glass. The notches of the cutter work exceptionally well on most inside curves. Notice the additional score lines I have added to remove unwanted glass.

1. *Using either your pliers or the teeth of your glasscutter, start by removing the piece closest to the edge of your pattern, as shown at right.*

2. *By adding all these score lines, you easily remove scrap when the curves are not that sharp, as shown.*

3. *Continue to remove pieces a little at a time.*

4. *Work one piece at a time. Don't try to rush this process. It doesn't always go smoothly.*

Additional score lines on inside curves provide a good way to remove a little glass at a time.

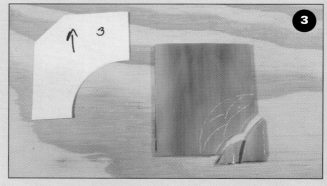

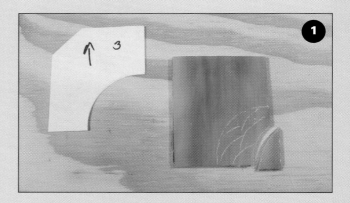

On difficult inside curves, this method is suited well to allow you to remove glass a little at a time. Because glass has a tendency to want to break in straight lines instead of following a curve, it is best to remove a little at a time.

Continue to work with these steps until you feel comfortable with the pressure required to make a good score and remove glass waste cleanly. Practice on following your pattern as accurately as possible with your cutter. The more accurate you become, the less grinding you will need and the better the end results.

Getting down to the final pieces.

Save all the pieces that you have cut out in this exercise. You will need them later when we cover the sections on grinding, copper foiling, and soldering.

Caution: *After removing the excess glass, your pieces are left with very sharp edges opposite the original score line. Instructions on how to remove the sharp edges will be demonstrated in the Why Grind? section, page 47. For now, be very careful handling these pieces of glass and store them in a safe place.*

It's not uncommon for more than one piece to break off at a time, as long as it follows the score line.

Maintenance

Your cutter needs little care. Occasionally, you can lubricate the wheel with a small drop of light general-purpose oil or kerosene.

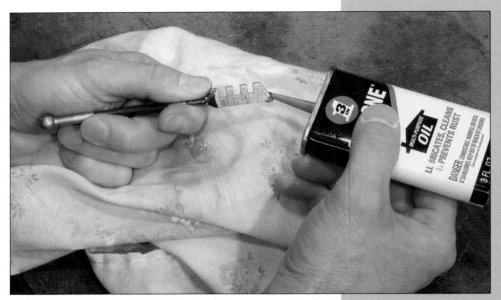

All you need is a little lubricant to keep your cutter in good shape.

Make sure it penetrates the whole wheel, then wipe off the excess oil and store away in the sleeve, if one is supplied.

Another way to keep it lubricated is to store the cutter in a little bit of kerosene, just enough to cover the wheel.

Make sure to wipe off the wheel prior to using it.

Cutter is stored in kerosene and occasionally dipped in the fluid during a lot of scoring.

Why Grind?

Grinding is an important step in glasswork. Without it, you risk a chance of cutting yourself, tearing your copper foil, or having your pieces not fit properly.

After breaking away the excess glass from your pattern piece, the bottom edge of glass (opposite the side of the score line) is left with a very sharp, jagged edge. This jagged edge needs to be ground off prior to copper foiling.

A piece in desperate need of grinding.

The edge that followed the score line will not be sharp or jagged because when excess glass is removed, the break follows the score line, leaving it dull. There is usually no need to grind this already dull score line. I'm not saying you will never need to grind the scored edge. Sometimes the break may not completely follow your score line, leaving it jagged, or your pattern may not be cut precisely and in need of a little grinding to make it fit better.

Safety

While grinding, small pieces of glass occasionally chip off in all directions. For this reason, it is recommended not to have others around when grinding. At the very least, have others keep a good distance away or wear safety glasses.

If you do not have a face shield on your grinder, safety glasses are recommended while grinding. Face shields are usually standard equipment, but if your grinder doesn't come with one, you can usually purchase a universal one that can be attached.

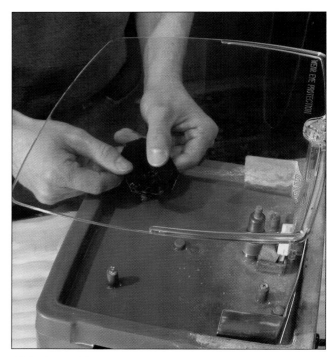

This face shield came with this grinder.

Lighting is another essential element in practicing good safety while grinding. You need to clearly see the edge of glass at all times so as not to grind a finger or accidentally move off the pattern.

Choosing a Head

The diamond head is the only type of head available for the grinder. It comes along with the grinder as a general-purpose head. You can, however, purchase a different diameter head if you desire. As an example, note the photo below, where you can see a smaller add-on head on top of my general purpose one.

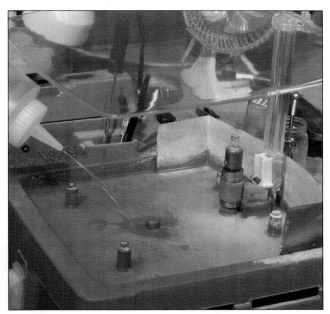

Water reservoir keeping the sponge wet.

A diamond grinding head can cut through glass fast and will continue to cut as long as you hold your glass on it. Be careful not to grind too much, as you risk a good chance of your pieces not fitting together properly.

The Role of Water

Before you grind, make sure the grinder reservoir contains the proper amount of water (as recommended by the grinder manufacturer). Add enough water so the sponge is sitting in it. The idea is to ensure there is enough to keep the glass cool.

Keeping the grinding wheel wet will minimize some of the flying glass, helps keep the glass cool to help prevent breaking, and helps move the glass dust particles away from the piece you are grinding.

When using an additional (smaller diameter) grinding head attachment, it will be necessary to apply water directly to it, since it will not reach the grinders reservoir.

Optional smaller wheel out of reach of water supply.

This optional attachment comes in handy when working with very tight inside curves.

The Procedure

If your project does not consist of a lot of pieces, cut out all your pieces first and then grind them all, leaving them all ready to be foiled at once. If there are multiple pieces, however, you may consider grinding a few at a time so that you are not grinding for hours on end.

After cutting, I like to group all my pieces to their shapes and line them up for grinding.

1. *Using both hands, firmly hold onto the glass piece and slowly approach the grinding wheel at an angle of about 10 degrees, as shown below, to grind off the jagged bottom edge only.*

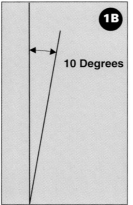

10 Degrees

Approach slowly and at a slight angle to the grinding wheel.

2. *Gently touching the piece to the grinding wheel, apply light pressure against the grinder. If you contact the grinder too quickly, the wheel could grab the glass, tossing it out of your hands.*

You will feel a little tug as the glass touches the wheel.

Tip: *If you hear the grinder motor slowing down, you're probably applying too much pressure. Just back off a little. You will have more control, get better results and your grinder will last longer if you let the grinding wheel do the work slowly.*

3. *Carefully guide the piece around all the edges while grinding off just enough glass as not to distort the actual pattern shape but to remove all the sharp edges. Try to keep a slightly more than 90-degree angle with your piece. By maintaining this angle, your pieces will have a better chance of fitting together properly.*

Try to maintain this angle throughout.

4. *After grinding, look at the piece closely, making sure you have gotten all the sharp edges.*

Above: Two pieces that show before and after grinding. Notice how only one edge is ground.

Make sure to get all the water and glass dust off each piece as soon as you're done grinding.

Because you are just starting out, compare your ground piece to the original pattern. If it appears to differ from the original pattern, grind where necessary so that you have a better match to your pattern. The closer the piece matches the pattern, the better the finished pieces will fit. The better the fit, the thinner your solder lines will be and you won't end up with unwanted gaps between your pieces.

After the grinding stage, closely inspect each piece, making sure you didn't miss any sharp edges. Then wipe each piece dry with a soft, lint-free cloth, as copper foil sticks better to a clean, dry piece of glass.

After grinding, check to see how the pieces fit together before putting copper foil around each.

Other Considerations

When you have completed the grinding process, you can leave the water in the grinder reservoir. Periodically, you will have to add additional water as it evaporates or gets used up in the grinding process. After a lot of grinding, the reservoir will accumulate fine dust-like particles of glass, so an occasional cleaning to remove these will be necessary.

Besides an occasional cleaning, there's no additional maintenance needed, but do be sure to check with the manufacturers recommendations.

When working on large projects with many pieces, it is best to grind pieces from one small area at a time so that you can place the finished pieces together in your pattern to see how well they fit before copper foiling.

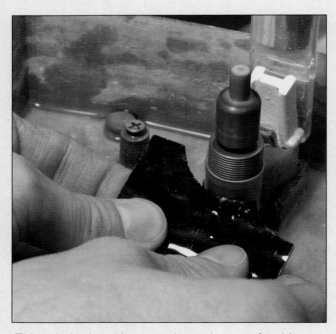

This grinder head is more than adequate for this piece.

Based on how well the pieces fit, this is the time you can grind more if necessary. As mentioned earlier, if you follow your pattern design precisely, you probably won't have to do any additional grinding.

Water added to this small piece helps with the grinding process.

As you develop your skills, your designs will naturally get more complicated. At that time, you will find the add-on head a welcome accessory. The only problem with this type of head is that it won't reach your water supply. Using your water bottle, add a little water to the small grinder head before you start. I also like to wet the piece that I'm grinding.

If the piece requires a lot of grinding, stop and add water when it looks like the grinder is starting to dry.

Like all steps in working with stained glass, grinding is not that difficult. It just takes practice.

Copper Foiling

So, what is copper foiling? Putting it simply, it is the process by which the entire edge of glass is covered with a thin piece of copper. These thin copper strips make it possible to connect your pieces of glass together, using solder.

Warning: Do not attempt to copper foil your pieces before you have completed the grinding stage.

In the past, you could only get copper foil in thin flat sheets of copper, similar to a sheet of paper. Each sheet would have to be cut into strips with a scissors to match the width of your glass. Applying the foil was much more difficult then, since crimping the edges was the only way the foil could be made to stick to the glass piece. It was a constant challenge trying to keep the foil attached!

With the invention of copper foil tape and its variety of available widths and thicknesses, foiling became a much easier task. The tape contains an adhesive side that easily adheres to the glass piece, making it less likely to slip when soldering.

The Procedure

1. *Using glass pieces that already have been cut and ground, begin the foiling process by first peeling away a small section of backing (about 2") from your roll of copper foil tape.*

Pieces cut and ground ready for foil.   Preparing the foil.

2. *With a cut and ground glass piece in hand, start foiling by placing the sticky side of the tape on one edge of the glass, making sure the foil is lined up as evenly as possible on both sides. I have found that starting in the middle of a long straight section of a pattern works best for me. Experiment with beginning the tape at different areas on the edge to find what works best for you.*

Start just before a corner or in the middle of a piece.

3. Continue smoothing the foil tape around the entire edge of your glass piece, as shown in the progression of photos below.

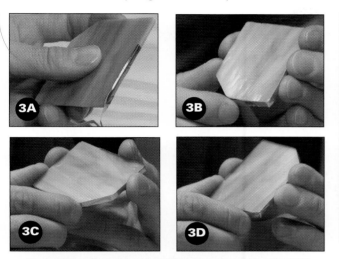

Tip: Copper foil is not very thick, so pulling it too hard may cause it to tear. If it does tear, you can easily repair it by overlapping the tear ⅛" or so, and then continuing.

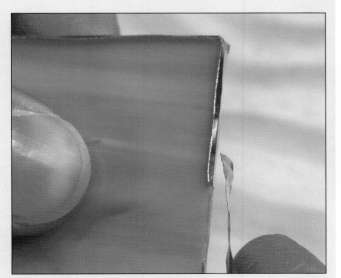

If foil gets torn in the middle of foiling, overlap a little and continue on.

4. Once you have foiled around the piece, overlap the beginning foil edge by about ⅛", as shown below.

Overlap, but keep the tape evenly lined up.

5. Lightly crimp the tape to the glass with your finger as you continue foiling. (You will be smoothing it out later).

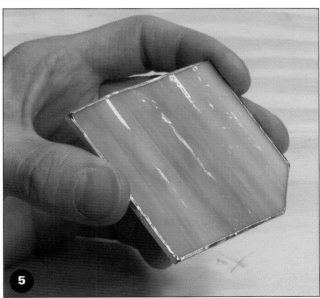

Lightly crimp the foil on the edges.

6. *Using the back of your thumbnail as shown, flatten both sides of your foil down to complete the process. Getting the tape to lie as flat as possible will make it less likely to snag the tip of the soldering iron when applying the solder. A smooth tape also adheres to the glass better, keeping it from falling off while handling the piece prior to soldering.*

Use your thumbnail to smooth out the foil, as shown in 6A, to achieve a completely foiled piece (6B).

Continue to practice foiling on the rest of your practice pieces until you feel somewhat comfortable with all the steps. As you foil each piece, set them aside. Avoid stacking them together; the taped edges have a tendency to catch on each other. This could result in pulling or tearing the foil away from your piece.

When working on a project, it's a good idea to have all your pieces foiled before moving on to soldering. That is, if you are working on a smaller project. For a large project, you may want to work with small sections at a time, cutting, grinding, foiling, and then spot soldering the pieces together.

A Word About Inside Curves

So far, we have been working only with basic geometric shapes (squares, rectangles, etc.). Working with patterns that have inside curves presents more of a challenge than outside curves or straight lines. This is true in cutting, grinding, and foiling.

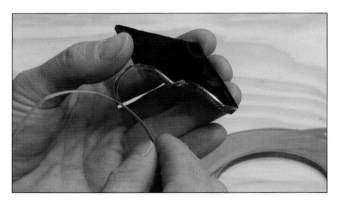

Inside curves can sometimes be a little challenging.

Inside curves have a tendency to tear the foil when making the inside bend. Practice is the only way to learn how copper foil works with different types of curves. Some of the projects included in this book have patterns that include some easy inside curves. For now, keep practicing on the practice patterns created earlier. That way, you will have mastered enough of the basics to help you get through the inside curves more successfully later on.

Soldering

After copper foiling your glass pieces, you need a means of joining them together. Melting solder onto the copper foil joints and then letting it cool provides the so-called glue to hold your pieces together.

You can compare solder to the thread used in quilt-making. Where the thread is used to combine patterns of cloth together, solder is used to join your foiled pieces of glass together.

Soldering Iron Safety

Because the fumes from melting lead solder are toxic and hazardous to your health and because the solder iron can heat up to a high enough temperature to start a fire, here are some simple safety tips to follow:

• Make sure you have a well-ventilated area.
• Keep your work surface clean and uncluttered.
• Use a fan to move fumes away from you while soldering.
• Never leave your soldering iron unattended.
• Keep your soldering iron on its holder while it is heating up or when not in use for short periods of time (a holder is usually supplied). If it did not come with a holder, it is a must to get one.
• After handling solder, make sure to wash your hands.

Soldering iron on a typical holder.

Maintenance

Very little maintenance is needed with your soldering iron. The key is really in keeping it clean.

Periodically clean the tip of your iron by wiping it off on a steel wool pad.

Gently wipe the soldering iron tip on steel wool pad.

Keeping the tip clean helps the solder to flow onto the foil better and gives the soldering iron a longer life span.

Getting Started

In an earlier section of this book, you practiced cutting, grinding, and copper foiling. We will be using some of the pieces you created earlier to help work our way through soldering.

Once your soldering iron is plugged in, how do you know when it's ready? You can test your iron by touching a piece of solder to the iron tip. If the solder melts easily when it touches the tip, your iron is ready. It shouldn't take more than a few minutes to heat up. If your soldering iron is left on too long without use, it can become overheated, which will cause the solder to roll off the tip instead of melting onto it. If the iron becomes overheated, let it set unplugged for a minute or two.

Solder melts easily when iron is ready.

Tip: *While laying your patterns out, remember that stained glass usually has one side smoother than the other (as opposed to clear glass where both sides are smooth). When working with stained glass, start by laying out your pieces with the smooth side up.*

Basic Soldering

While your iron is heating up, locate some of the foiled pieces you made earlier. Use at least three pieces that fit nicely together. Square or rectangular pieces will also work fine.

1. *Lay your pieces out on your work surface.*

Pieces lined up on your work surface.

2. *To help prevent your pieces from moving around while soldering, place pins or nails along the outside edges of your project, as shown in the progression of photos at right. The hardness of your work surface will determine which will work better. You should be using the board you purchased as your work surface, especially for this section.*

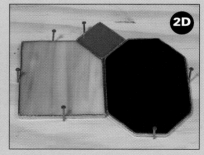

Securing the pieces in place.

Caution: *While applying solder, the glass will become very hot. When you need to turn your piece over or move it when done, allow enough time for it to cool down.*

3. *With your pieces in place and secure, apply flux along the copper foiled joints. Apply enough to sufficiently cover the joint, as flux helps the solder to adhere to the copper foil and flow evenly along the joints.*

Applying flux to the joints.

4. *Unroll about 6" to 8" of solder, or break off a piece from the roll, about 10" long.*

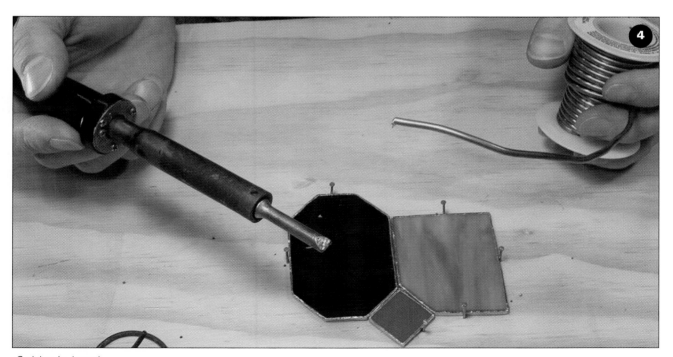

Solder in hand.

5. With your solder in one hand and the iron in the other, approach the joint.

Iron and solder ready to apply.

6. Just before contacting the foil, touch the solder to the end of the iron. As the solder melts onto the joint, continue at a steady pace as long as the solder melts easily. If it appears the solder is not melting very easily, slow your pace down or stop and let the iron heat back up again.

As the solder melts, keep a slow even pace.

Tip: *Allow the iron to stay in one spot just long enough to melt the solder to the foil. Leaving the iron in one spot too long can overheat the area, causing the glass to break or the solder to melt between the joints to the other side.*

If the glass breaks, there is little you can do but replace the broken piece with a new one. This is one reason to keep your original patterns in a safe place.

If the solder melts through to the other side, leave that area and allow it to cool down before returning to add more solder. When you return, you may need to add more flux and just enough solder to fill the joint.

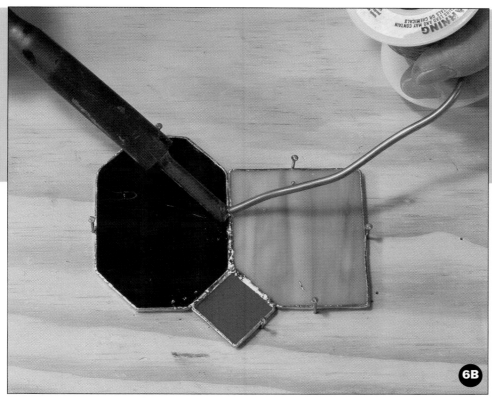

Tip: Corrosion may occur if the copper foil is exposed to the air too long, making it very difficult for the solder to stick.

Partially completed joint.

7. To get the edges of the foil, you will have to remove the pins or nails so they won't be in your way.

Make sure all the copper foil is covered, including the outside edges.

Spot Soldering

Often used in lamp-making, spot soldering is a method of temporarily connecting pieces in place by using small amounts of solder, which allows minor adjustments to be made.

When creating lamps, you will most likely be working on a form of some kind. As you add pieces, you will need to temporarily hold them in place to keep them from sliding off your form.

Here is the entire process:

1. Begin by pinning your pieces in place on the form, as shown below.

Pieces pinned in place ready for spot soldering.

2. Add flux before the actual spot soldering commences.

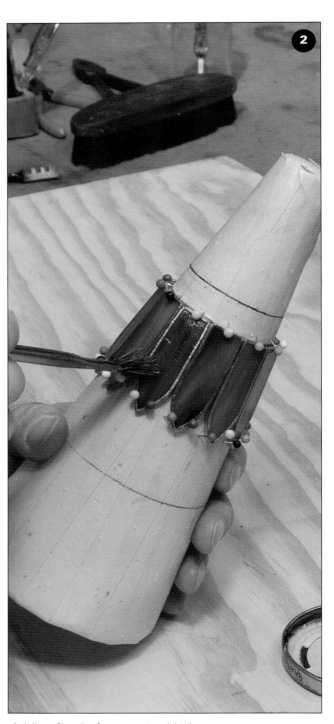

Adding flux before spot soldering.

3. *Start spot soldering both at the top and bottom of each piece, as shown below. Add just enough to hold them in place.*

4. *As you spot solder, you can then remove the pins as you continue around the form.*

Apply just enough solder to hold your pieces in place.

Remove pins as you spot solder your pieces in place.

Periodically, while working on forms like these, you will need to make adjustments to your pieces to keep them in line with your design. By melting the small solder spots (freeing the pieces), you can then make your adjustments. When finished, spot solder them back in their new position.

Step-by-step examples of this will be demonstrated in the lamp project section.

Intermediate Soldering

Intermediate soldering is the practice of applying solder to both sides of your project prior to the finishing stage.

Here, I will walk you through the procedure as it would be used on a flat-panel piece, but be aware that it can also be used in lamp-making. When it is used for lamp-making, you will already have all your pieces spot soldered in place, so you can skip the first two steps and start with step 3.

You should be familiar with the patterns I have used here, as they are a combination of two of the three patterns from the beginning of the book.

Here's how to put it all together:

1. Lay out the foiled pieces in the pattern you want for the finished piece. Make sure the smoother side of glass is facing up.

2. Use pins, small nails, or small strips of wood to keep your pieces in place on your form, as shown.

Tip: *Small strips of wood work best when working on a large project or on a project with a lot of pieces. When laying your wood out, it helps to use a square to make sure your wood is at a right-angle.*

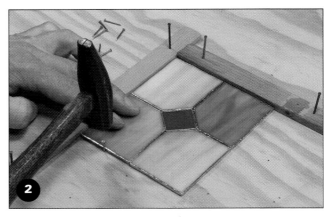

Strips of wood used to create a right-angle. Nails are used along the outside edge to keep your pieces in place while soldering.

3. Apply enough flux to sufficiently cover all the copper foil. If the project you're working on is large, concentrate on small areas at a time.

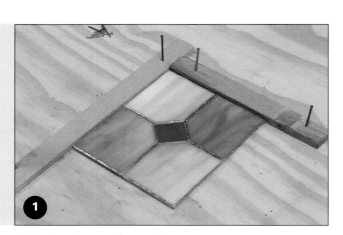

Foiled and ready for solder.

Cover all joints with flux.

4. With your iron hot, use a slow and steady motion to apply the solder, as shown below.

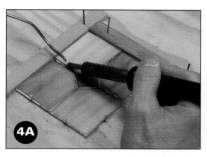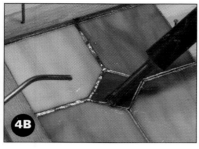

Start at any outside edge and move slowly and steadily.

5. Continue adding solder, making sure to cover all the joints, as shown below.

6. Caution: Your glass may be very hot at this time. With this in mind, carefully loosen the pins or nails, but leave the strips of wood in place. Turn your project over.

Ready to solder the other side.

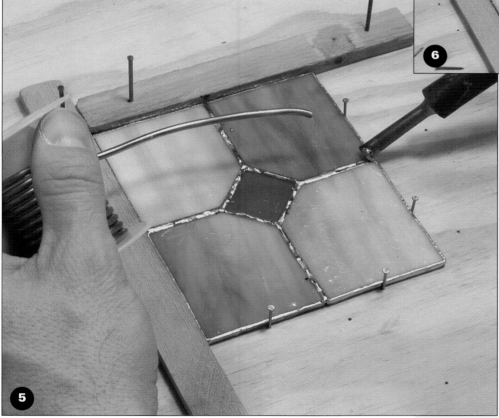

Make sure you have all the joints covered.

7. Once again, secure your project in place with nails or pins and repeat steps 3 through 5. This will be the only time you need to apply solder on the backside of a piece like this, since the back will not be displayed. The finished appearance on the back is not as critical as on the displayed side.

Tip: While soldering, you will need to occasionally lift your iron from the joints as you add more solder or while making your way around your project. When lifting your iron from your project, the solder can create very sharp points, which can be dangerous when cleaning or applying a finish. Shown below is an example of what some of the spikes might look like before smoothing.

Dangerous spikes of solder.

8. After you have covered all the joints with solder, go back and apply additional flux and smooth out any sharp points or rough areas. Melt the solder that needs correcting and then quickly lift your iron as you work to smooth the rough spots. The solder will usually lay back down, nicely rounding off and eliminating these problem areas.

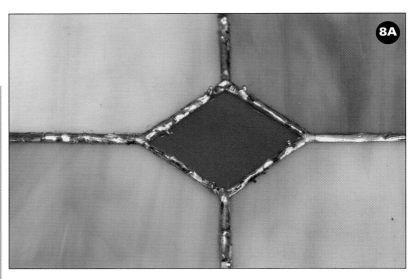

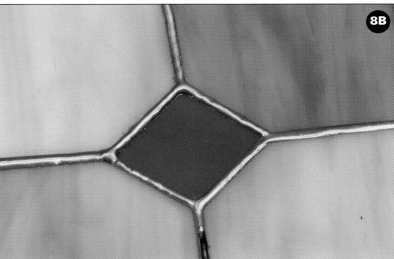

Before and after touching up.

Finish Soldering

Finish soldering is the final step in the soldering process. The objective during finish soldering is to smooth out the solder, creating even, well-rounded lines.

Here's how:

1. *Place your previously soldered project, good side up (the side that will be displayed) on your work surface.*

Display side up.

2. *Secure your project to your workbench using pins, nails, or small wood pieces as before.*

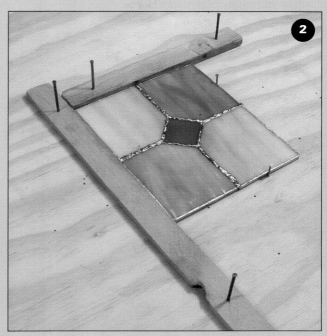

Piece held in place once again.

3. *Apply flux over all the solder joints.*

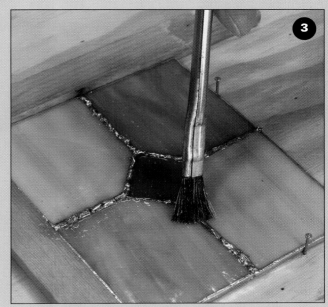

Reapplying flux.

4. When solder iron is sufficiently hot (solder melts easily when touched to the tip), start adding anywhere on an outside edge where necessary. Move with a steady pace, melting the solder as you go.

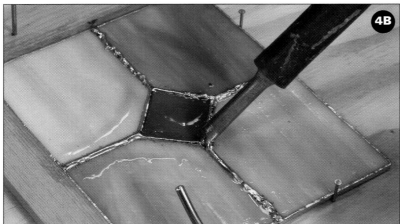

Tip: The pace that you maintain in step 4 will be determined by how well your soldering iron retains the correct temperature to melt solder efficiently. Remember that the iron continually loses heat as you solder. The faster your pace, the more solder you melt, and the quicker the heat loss. Work at a pace that allows the solder to melt easily. You want to leave behind an even, well rounded flow of solder. Also be careful not to stay in one spot too long, as you could overheat an area, melting your solder through the joint to the other side. If this happens, leave the area, allowing it to cool a little, then come back and add additional solder. Remove any excess solder that may melt through when you are finished. Solder that melts through is not as common on flat panel projects. Where you will usually see this problem is in lamp-making, where there is nothing on the backside to prevent solder from melting through like the workbench does on flat projects. You will see additional examples of this in the section on lamp-making.

5. When all the solder lines are smooth and even and the piece has cooled sufficiently for you to touch, turn the piece over to check if any solder melted through to the other side. If needed, apply additional flux to the areas where the solder has melted through.

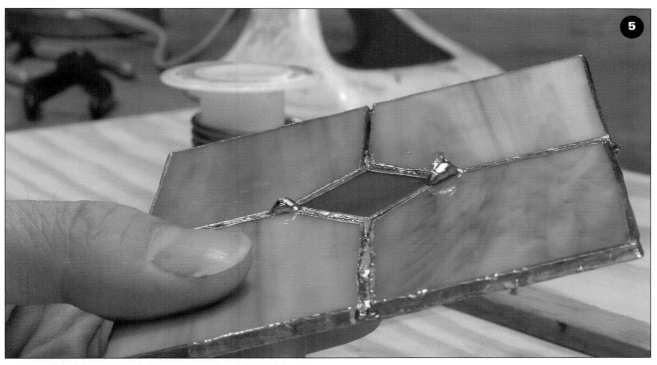

Blobs of solder melted through to the other side.

6. While holding your project at a slant, carefully use your hot soldering iron to melt the mound of solder enough so it falls to your worktable. Be careful not to drip any solder onto your hand.

7. After all the excess solder has been removed, add more flux and solder, if necessary, and touch up the areas where the solder was just removed.

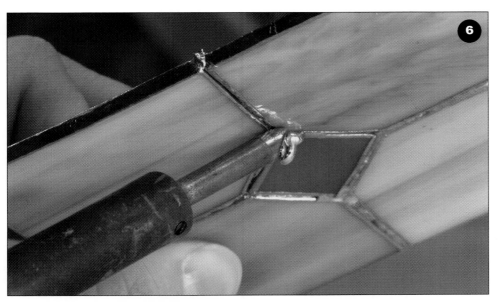

Proper way to remove excess solder.

Tinning

Tinning is the process of applying (melting) a very thin coat of solder to the surface of any type of metal that can be soldered. You might also describe it as being similar to "plating" a piece of metal. Once you try it, it is not as difficult as it sounds.

Tinning a brass lamp ring is a necessary step prior to attaching it to your stained glass lamp. This process allows the solder to easily melt between the two surfaces that already have solder on them. If you don't tin the ring, there's a good chance the glass will break from holding the iron in one area too long while trying to apply solder, or your solder will not melt to the ring at all. The reason such a problem occurs is because the ring acts as a "heat sink," which is a device used to help dissipate heat from an area. It is similar to the radiator in your car, which is used to keep your engine cool while dissipating heat.

In this process, you will only be tinning the inside of the ring, using a minimal amount of solder.

Here's how it is done:

1. *Because the ring is going to become extremely hot, begin by grasping it with pliers, as shown below.*

Pliers safely holding the ring.

2. *With ring safely in pliers, apply a generous amount of flux to the ring.*

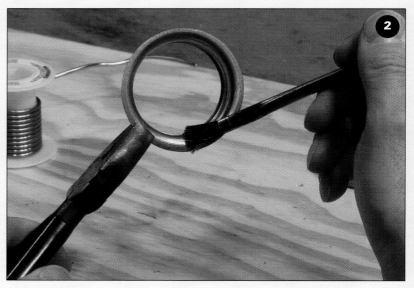

Apply flux.

3. Because the solder melts onto the ring better if you heat the ring up before applying solder, lay your soldering iron directly on the ring for about a minute while holding it in the pliers, as shown below.

Preheating ring with soldering iron.

4. Melt some solder on the tip of your iron and touch the iron to the ring, as shown.

Iron with small amount of solder.

Safety Tip: In step 4, the hot iron will probably cause the flux to smoke a little. Don't forget to use your fan to move these fumes away from you.

5. Move the solder around evenly, spreading a thin coat of it over the surface. Creating an even coat will leave enough solder on the ring surface to connect to the lampshade without overheating the glass in the process.

Almost done.

Before and after tinning.

Attaching a Lamp Ring

After the ring is properly tinned, the final step to the process is to attach it.

1. Lay tinned ring upside-down and flat on your work surface. Remember, if you just finished tinning, it will still be very hot, so handle with care.

Ready to set in place.

2. Turn your (completed) lampshade upside-down on top of the ring. Line it up evenly spaced around the ring.

Shade on top of ring.

3. Apply additional flux to prepare it for spot soldering.

Applying flux.

4. Spot solder the ring to the lamp base, as shown below, keeping it centered.

Ring spot soldered in place.

5. Once you have the ring spot soldered to the shade, carefully pick it up, holding it so you can easily apply additional solder to finish the attachment.

Add solder to complete the attachment.

6. Finish by rounding off your solder smoothly and evenly, as if you were working with any typical solder joint.

7. Repeat soldering on the inside of the lamp and remember to inspect for solder spikes or excess solder, and smooth them down also.

Lamp-Making Form

A form is used in lamp-making not only as the foundation providing the overall shape of your lamp, but also as a necessary element during the construction phase. It holds your glass pieces in place (with the help of pins) prior to soldering. The advanced artist can make his or her own form out of sheets of polystyrene and is limited only by his or her imagination.

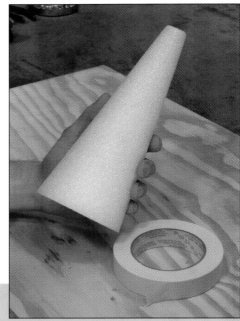

Standard form 9" tall and 3¾"-diameter base.

Preparing Your Form

Your form will be your foundation for lining up your foiled pieces just before soldering. The form is critical in making sure your pieces will fit and what your lamp will look like when finished. Once you have prepared the form with the following steps, it will be ready to make several lampshades on.

1. Start by placing strips of ordinary masking tape approximately 1" or 2" longer than the form from top to bottom, as shown in the progression of photos below.

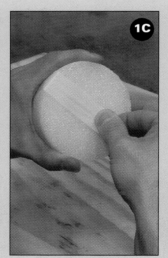

Be sure to apply the tape in a smooth and straight manner.

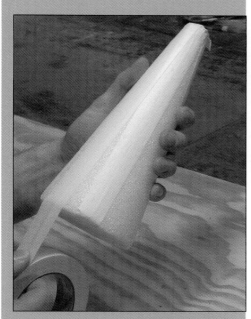

Overlap, but not more than once.

2. *As you apply the tape, occasionally smooth it down with your hands. You want a flat even surface to work on.*

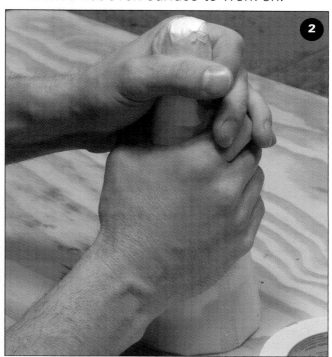

3. *As you continue to apply tape, the center on the bottom will start to build up, causing your form to tip or wobble while working on it. To offset wobbliness, indent the center of the form with your thumb so your form stands up straight.*

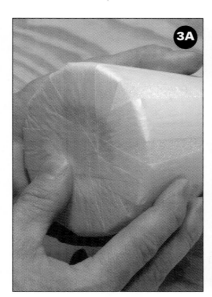

Indent the center with your thumb.

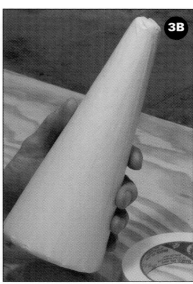

Form completely taped.

4. Once the form is completely taped, place a lamp ring onto the top of the form and snug it in place.

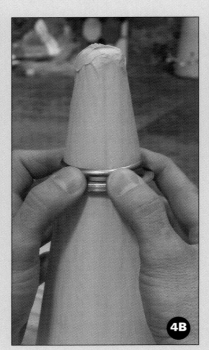

Ring should fit snug on the form.

5. With ballpoint pen or felt-tipped marker, follow the inside of the ring, making a line completely around the form.

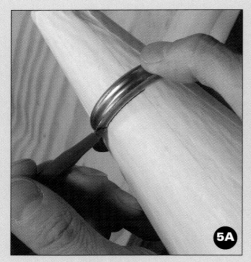

Using the ring as your guide.

Use the outside of the rim of the ring (not the inside) as your guide.

6. Remove the ring to show the reference lines for the first row of pieces.

The form is now ready to have pieces added.

Congratulations! Once you have made it this far, you have only the final and easiest process in working in stained glass: cleaning and applying patina finish.

Cleaning and Applying Patina

In order for the patina to cover your solder evenly, you will need to remove all the flux and residue from the foil tape and glass. For best results, clean and apply the patina as soon as you're done soldering.

1. *Fill a bucket with hot water and an ample amount of grease-fighting laundry soap.*

2. *Using a small scrub brush, thoroughly clean both sides of the entire piece. Make sure you get all the residue off. It is imperative you get the piece very clean.*

3. Wipe your project dry.

4. *Wearing rubber gloves, use a brush or soft rag to apply the patina, per manufacturer's instructions, until all the solder is covered.*

5. *Wash your project again to remove any patina from the glass.*

Wear gloves when applying patina.

Flat panel before applying patina ...   *and after.*

Fan lamp before applying patina ...   *and after.*

 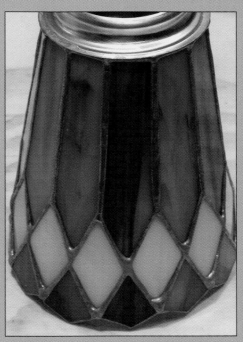

Lampshade before applying patina ...   *and after.*

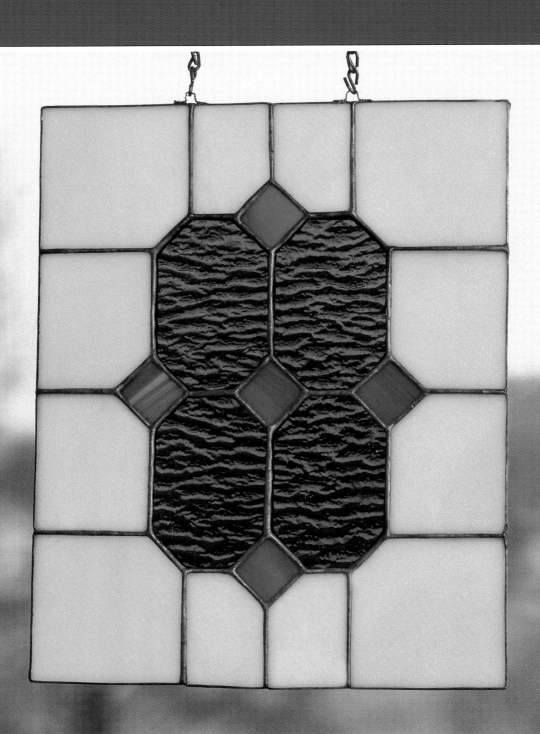

This project is a simple, yet nice-looking flat-panel piece. What you have learned throughout this book will all come together when making this first project.

I will provide instructions on cutting, foiling, grinding, and soldering one piece through both written steps and photos, and then you will repeat the process for each of the other pieces.

After you have completed this project, these same steps can be applied to any project regardless of size or design.

So let's get started!

Glass looks different with light behind it.

Tip: Feel free to deviate from the colors shown, but keep in mind that when picking out glass, carefully hold up the pieces to a light source. Holding the piece to light allows you to see if the true color of the glass will blend with each sheet. It will also give you a better representation of how your project will look when completed.

Preparing the Paper Pattern

1. *Looking at the pattern on page 91, notice that each piece is numbered and the arrows indicate the direction of the grain. If you would like to change the look of your piece and feel comfortable in doing so, you may change the direction of the grain to suit your tastes.*

2. *Trace the pattern pieces onto paper.*

3. *After tracing the patterns onto paper, cut them out. These paper patterns will serve as the templates for cutting your glass.*

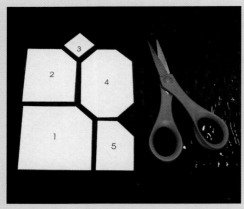

All pattern pieces cut and ready to get started.

Cutting the Pieces

1. *Begin by first realizing how many pieces of each pattern piece you will need to cut from the glass. Here are the number of pieces needed:*

- *Four of #1 from caramel glass*
- *Four of #2 from caramel glass (two cut with the pattern facing up or "side A" and two with the pattern facing with the opposite side up or "side B")*
- *Five of #3 from orange glass*
- *Four of #4 from amber ripple glass*
- *Four of #5 from caramel glass (two cut with the pattern facing up or "side A" and two with the pattern facing with the opposite side up or "side B")*

2. *Reduce the size of your glass to a more manageable and safer size to work with. By doing so, you will also get more pieces cut with less waste.*

3. *With your ruler, size up your pattern on each end of the glass.*

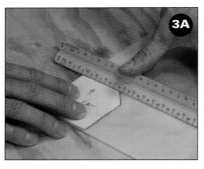 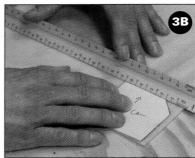

4. *Draw a line along the ruler with your marking pen.*

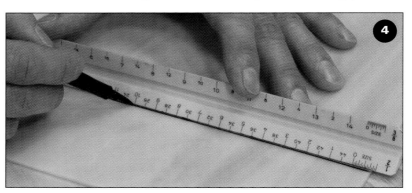

5. *Score along the line.*

6. *Quickly snap the piece and you're ready to start cutting your patterns out.*

7. *Line up your pattern on one end and make your first score line.*

8. *With a good score line, you should be able to separate the pattern with your hands, as shown.*

9. *When scoring smaller pieces, use the teeth of the cutter to remove the scraps.*

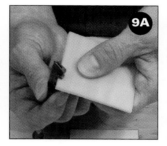
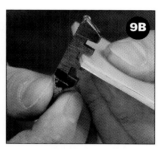
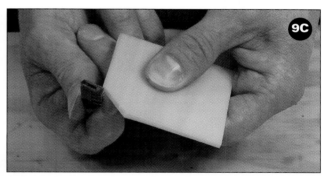

10. *When the piece is done, put it aside until all pieces are cut. Repeat steps 1 through 9 for all remaining pattern pieces.*

Tip: *If you should run out of glass with your initial reduced piece, just size up another piece from the sheet and continue until all patterns are cut out.*

Grinding the Pieces

Before you begin, make sure you have water in your grinder reservoir.

Tip: It's not a bad idea to organize your pieces in a fashion that makes your grinding run more efficiently. I like to stack all my pieces along one side of my grinder so I can get to them easily. I also use an old metal pan to keep my pieces in after I grind them. This keeps the workspace dry, clean, and organized.

Pieces stacked along the side of the grinder while grinding.

Pan used to hold the wet pieces.

1. Using both hands, firmly hold one of the cut glass pattern pieces and slowly approach the grinding wheel at an angle of about 10 degrees to grind off the jagged bottom edge only. If necessary, refer to the photo for step 1 on page 50 in the Why Grind? section.

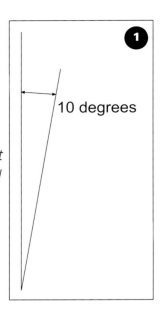

10 degrees

2. Gently touching the piece to the grinding wheel, apply light pressure against the grinder. If you contact the grinder too quickly, the wheel could grab the glass, tossing it out of your hands. This step is illustrated in the step 2 photo on page 50 in the Why Grind? section.

3. Carefully guide the piece around all the edges while grinding off just enough glass. Try to keep a slightly more than 90-degree angle with your piece. By maintaining this angle, your pieces will have a better chance of fitting together properly. Again, if a visual is needed here, this step is illustrated in the step 3 photo on page 50 in the Why Grind? section.

4. After grinding, examine the piece, making sure you have gotten all the sharp edges.

5. Repeat steps 1 through 4 for all pieces.

6. *After you have all the pieces ground, wipe the water and glass dust off. It's difficult to foil unless they are clean.*

Make sure each piece is clean before you foil them.

7. *Lay all your pieces out in your expected final pattern to check for a proper fit and grind any pieces that do not fit properly. Grind only where absolutely necessary.*

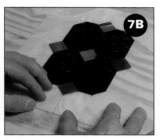

Check to see how well your pieces fit together by laying them out before moving on to copper foiling.

Foiling the Pieces

1. *Begin with centering one glass piece on the sticky side of copper foil tape. Remember to start by peeling away a small section of tape from its backing (about 2").*

Press the tape to the edge as you move around the piece.

2. *Keep your foil as even as possible on both sides, smooth down the foil around the entire edge of your glass piece with the help of your thumbnail. Lightly crimp the tape to the glass as you go.*

Using your thumbnail, flatten the edges down.

3. *Once you have foiled around the piece, overlap the beginning foil edge by about ⅛".*

4. *Using the back of your thumbnail, flatten both sides of your foil down to complete the process.*

5. *Repeat steps 1 through 5 for all remaining project pieces.*

Soldering the Pieces

1. After all the pieces are foiled, lay them out on your workbench.

Pieces all foiled and ready for the next step in the soldering process.

2. Nail two small strips of wood onto your workbench in a right angle with the help of a square. Allow enough room so your entire pattern will fit.

3. Assemble your foiled glass pieces in the pattern of the completed project, as shown in the progression of photos here. Start with the good side of each piece facing up.

4. Using two more strips of wood or nails as I did, secure the two remaining edges of the project so your pieces will not move when soldering.

Here, nails were used to keep the pieces secure while soldering.

5. Apply flux to all the foil, as shown. While applying flux, have your soldering iron plugged in so it will be ready to solder when you are done.

Applying flux.

Safety Check: Don't forget to have your fan on to move the fumes away from you while you solder.

6. When your iron is hot enough, begin applying the solder to the joints, starting on any outside edge first. I like to hold onto the roll of solder, unrolling what I need as I go. Don't worry about getting your solder on perfectly because you will have to go over this side again, but do make sure to cover all the foil, even the very edges of your project. Covering all the foil will add strength to your joints and to your finished project. It is also beneficial when cleaning and applying your patina.

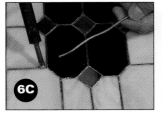
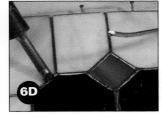

Start soldering on any outside edge and continue to the interior portions of the piece.

Tip: Remember not to stay in one area too long. If an area gets too hot, your solder may melt through to the other side. If this happens, leave the area and let it cool before you add more solder. The best advice I can give you on soldering is to move as quickly as possible. This will always give you the best results.

7. Once you have soldered the first side, remove your nails or strips of wood from two sides only and turn the glass over so you can solder the other side. Remember: Be careful as your glass may be very hot at this time.

Carefully turn your piece over.

8. With your wood strips still in place, add a nail or two to keep your glass secure.

9. Note areas on the piece where the solder has melted through the joints to the other side, as shown. Sometimes you will end up with globs of solder that you will have to remove.

Some solder coming through from the other side.

10. Flux once again and solder this side as you did the first side. Make sure to get all the foil covered— even on the edges. The photo below shows a good example of what the backside should look like. You don't need to get the well-rounded, even solder joints on the backside, unless you plan on your project being displayed from both sides.

12. Flux and solder the good side one more time. Move quickly and in a steady motion. If you don't get it looking just right, you can always go back and touch it up. Note the example in the photo of how a good side should look when completed. Notice the even, smooth lines of solder.

Smooth, well-rounded lines of solder.

Good soldering job for the backside.

11. Once you have completed the backside soldering, remove the nails as before and turn the piece over once again.

13. While your project is still warm, wipe off as much of the flux as possible. The longer you leave it on, the harder it will be to remove later.

Finished with soldering.

Finishing the Project

1. Fill a bucket with hot water and an ample amount of grease-fighting laundry soap.

2. Using a small scrub brush, thoroughly clean both sides of the entire piece. Make sure you get all of the residue off, as it is imperative you get the piece very clean.

3. Wipe your project dry.

4. Wearing rubber gloves, use a brush or soft rag to apply the patina per manufacturer's instructions until all the solder is covered.

5. Wash your project again to remove any patina from the glass.

Flat-Panel Pattern

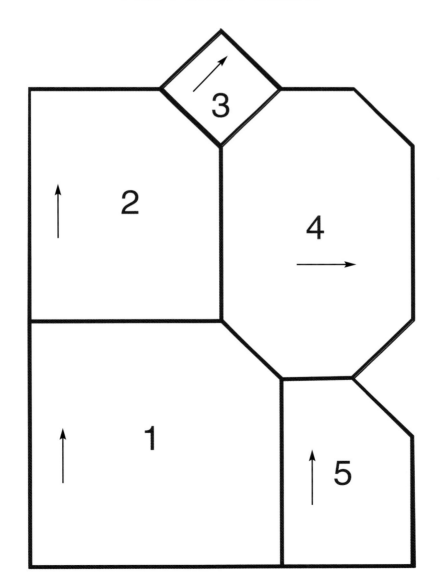

The fan is a uniquely different lamp. It's constructed similar to the flat panel, but the end product will be an incredible piece of art to cherish for many years. The glow this piece gives off in a dark room is definitely one-of-a-kind.

Although this piece can be displayed as a window hanging, it is best displayed in a stand similar to the one I use. This lamp base can be purchased from various stained glass suppliers, several of which are listed in the Resources section (page 124), at a cost of less than $30. If you have access to the Internet, try searching for "fan lamp bases."

Materials

- 1-square-foot cathedral red glass
- 1-square-foot wispy red/white combination glass
- 1-square-foot wispy red/caramel combination glass
- Lamp base
- 1 sheet each tracing paper, carbon paper, and plain white paper
- 1 roll 7/32"-wide x 1.25mm-thick copper foil
- Several stick pins or small nails
- 2 to 4 thin wood strips
- Flux and flux brush
- 1 lb. 50/50 solder
- 8-oz. bottle patina and cloth
- Water and water bottle (for grinding)
- Hot water, brush, laundry soap, and bucket (for cleaning)
- Glasscutter
- Grinder
- Soldering iron
- Pliers
- Rubber gloves
- Scissors
- Pencil
- Pattern (page 102)

Three variations of red glass.

Two of the three pieces; notice that there is quite a contrast between these pieces.

Typical fan lamp base.

Preparing the Paper Pattern

1. Looking at the pattern on page 102, notice that each piece is numbered and the direction of the grain noted.

2. Trace the pattern pieces onto paper.

3. After tracing the patterns onto paper, cut them out. These paper patterns will serve as the templates for cutting your glass.

Fan pattern.

Cutting the Pieces

Tip: *All the pattern pieces in this design are quite simple, with the exception of #1 and #2. What makes them more difficult are the long narrow points they come to. Don't be surprised if it takes a few tries to get your first piece cut out cleanly. I will do my best to describe the best way to do this with as little frustration as possible.*

1. Begin by first realizing how many pieces of each pattern piece you will need cut from the glass. Here is the number of pieces needed:
- Four of #1 from wispy red/white glass
- Four of #2 from wispy red/white glass
- Four of #3 from wispy red/caramel glass
- Four of #4 from wispy red/caramel glass
- Seven of #5 from cathedral red glass
- One of #6 from cathedral red glass
- One of #7 from cathedral red glass
- Eight of #8 from wispy red/caramel glass

2. Starting with pattern piece #2, reduce your wispy red/white glass to the size of the pattern and line it up on one end of the glass.

Pattern #2 lined up on the edge ready for scoring.

3. Even though your pattern stops short, make sure to run your score line straight out to the edge of the glass, as shown below.

First score line.

4. Continue to score the entire piece. Remember not to score over the same line twice, as you will dull your cutter sooner than you'd like.

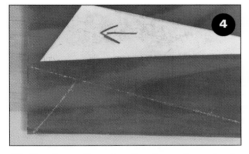

Notice how the shorter line stops just before touching the other score line.

5. Now that you have the pattern completely scored, remove the excess glass using one of the methods outlined in the sidebar on page 96 . When removing excess glass, it might not follow the score line the way you planned and may break in an unpredictable direction. Stay with it!

6. Use a glass piece cut from pattern #2 to obtain the proper angle to help cut out the pattern #1 pieces. Line #1 pattern piece up on the previous #2 score line, as shown. This is a perfect way to reduce waste and save glass.

Pattern #1 lined up on previous score line from pattern #2.

All scored and ready to remove scrap and then line up pattern #1 again.

7. Alternate pattern #1 and #2 as you score and cut so that you not only save glass but also end up with less cutting, since one side is already cut from the previous pattern.

8. Next, score and cut pattern #8.

Pattern completely scored.

9. *Use your hands to snap out the first piece, as shown.*

First and largest piece snapped out with my hands.

10. *Use the glasscutter to remove scrap around piece #8, as shown in the following sequence of photos.*

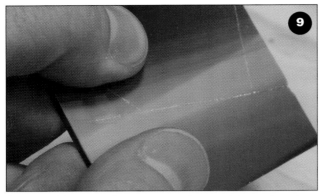

All scrap removed.

11. *Score, cut, and remove scrap from the remaining pattern.*

Removing Scrap

Here are several methods you can use when removing excess glass. I use them all at various times. Sometimes, it depends on the hardness of the glass (making one method more difficult to use than another). Since all glass is different, experiment with all of these methods.

Option 1: I like using my hands to remove glass whenever possible. If the glass can't be separated with a quick snap, you probably need to try another method. Forcing it to break will only result in injury.

Using just your hands. This does not work well on pieces much smaller than this.

Option 2: I line up the pliers on the edge of the score line, closer to one end, but not right on the edge. All glass reacts differently when scrap is removed. I have found that when using pliers, it is best to stay off-center to one end or the other. Working in the middle seems to give me more problems as does right on the edge of the glass.

Using your pliers to remove glass.

Option 3: Using the teeth of the cutter is probably my favorite way to remove scrap. In time, you will find it convenient to score and remove scrap quickly, having one tool in your hand to do both.

Using your glasscutter to remove scrap.

Your objective in removing scrap is to have this pile as small as possible. Smaller pile means less waste.

Typical scrap pile.

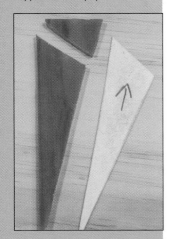

All scrap removed. That wasn't so bad!

Grinding the Pieces

1. Line up the glass pieces on the side of your grinder, making them easy to reach. Also be sure to have a pan ready to hold the wet pieces.

Pieces lined up ready to grind.

Notice the pan to hold the wet pieces of glass.

2. Using both hands, firmly hold one of the cut glass pattern pieces and slowly approach the grinding wheel at an angle of about 10 degrees to grind off the jagged bottom edge only. If necessary, refer to the photo for step 1 on page 50 in the Why Grind? section.

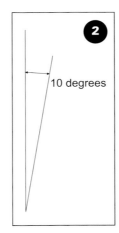

10 degrees

3. Gently touching the piece to the grinding wheel, apply light pressure against the grinder. If you contact the grinder too quickly, the wheel could grab the glass, tossing it out of your hands. This step is illustrated in the step 2 photo on page 50 in the Why Grind? section.

4. Carefully guide the piece around all the edges while grinding off just enough glass. Try to keep a slightly more than 90-degree angle with your piece. By maintaining this angle, your pieces will have a better chance of fitting together properly. Again, if a visual is needed here, this step is illustrated in the step 3 photo on page 50 in the Why Grind? section.

5. After grinding, examine the piece, making sure you have removed all the sharp edges.

6. Repeat steps 2 through 5 for all pieces.

7. After grinding make sure to wipe all the pieces thoroughly. You don't want any glass dust or water left on the pieces prior to foiling.

8. *When clean and dry, lay out the glass pieces in the design of your completed pattern, as shown in the progression of photos here. Check to see if there is any additional grinding that needs to be done prior to foiling. Look for any gaps or uneven lines. Your pieces should fit as tight as possible.*

Ready for foiling.

Foiling the Pieces

1. *Begin with centering one glass piece on the sticky side of copper foil tape. Remember to start by peeling away a small section of tape from its backing (about 2"). If necessary, refer to the photos for step 1 of the foiling instructions on pages 54-55 in the Copper Foiling section, for guidance.*

2. *Keep your foil as even as possible on both sides, smooth down the foil around the entire edge of your glass piece with the help of your thumbnail. Lightly crimp the tape to the glass as you go. Again, refer to the photos for step 1 of the foiling instructions, page 54, for guidance, if necessary.*

3. *Once you have foiled around the piece, overlap the beginning foil edge by about ⅛".*

4. *Using the back of your thumbnail, flatten both sides of your foil down to complete the process.*

5. *Repeat steps 1 through 5 for all remaining project pieces.*

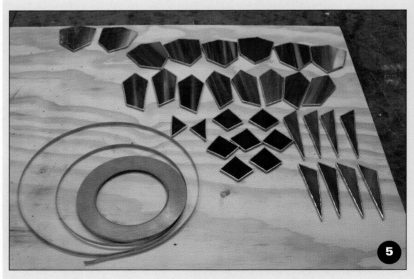

All pieces foiled and ready for soldering.

Soldering the Pieces

1. Before you lay your pattern out for soldering, nail a starter board on your workbench. Make sure to allow enough room for the entire project to fit.

2. Lay out your pattern pieces from the bottom of the design to the top, making sure all the pieces are laid out with the "good" side facing up.

Make sure all your pieces line up.

3. Line up a second strip of wood along the other side of your design, keeping it as close as possible to the glass without moving any pieces out of line. Nail the board in place.

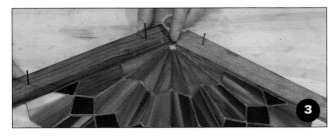

4. With fingers as shown, lightly tap on the top of the pieces to snug them in place. Make the adjustments needed so all your pattern lines match up.

Tap lightly on top to snug up your pieces.

Tip: Notice how the points of the very bottom pieces are not perfectly matched up. This is acceptable, since this portion of the fan will not be seen when placed in the base. If you plan on just hanging the piece, however, you can fill this void in with solder.

5. Once the pattern pieces are all in place, use small nails to keep the project from moving while you solder.

Small nails used to keep the pieces in place.

Safety Check: Position your fan to move the fumes away from you while you solder.

6. Apply flux to the copper foil.

Apply flux to sufficiently cover all the copper foil.

7. When your iron is ready, start soldering from the top to the bottom. Remember to move as quickly as possible for best results.

Smooth, steady motion.

8. Cover all the edges with solder to help keep the copper foil from tearing when cleaning or applying a patina.

Cover all edges with solder too.

9. Once you have soldered all the joints, turn your fan over. Be careful since the glass can be hot right after soldering.

Careful, it could be hot!

10. Line the fan back up to the strips of wood, as shown.

11. Add a couple of nails to keep the project from moving.

12. Flux and solder this side as with the previous side, taking care to also solder all the edges.

Covering all edges with solder.

13. Let the piece cool for a few minutes and add more flux to the edge, if needed. While carefully holding the fan on end, add solder along the outer edge.

Safety Check: Be very careful not to have your other hand directly under the iron while soldering.

Cover the outer edges, being careful not to drip solder on your hand.

14. Flip the fan over once again to the first side, place it back between the two strips of wood, and add a couple of nails to keep it from moving.

15. Apply flux again if necessary, or just use your flux brush to move around the flux that is already on it.

16. With solder iron, start again at the top and move your way down to the bottom, moving in a steady pace over the joints. If you need to add solder, do so. You want nice, rounded even lines of solder when done. Try to avoid building solder up where joints intersect.

Even and well-rounded lines of solder.

If an area gives you problems, leave it and come back when it cools down, adding more flux and solder if necessary.

17. Use a dry cloth and wipe off as much flux as possible so that cleaning will be easier.

Finishing Your Lamp

1. Fill a bucket with hot water and an ample amount of grease-fighting laundry soap.

2. Using a small scrub brush, thoroughly clean both sides of the entire piece. Make sure you get all of the residue off, as it is imperative you get the piece very clean.

3. Wipe your project dry.

4. Wearing rubber gloves, use a brush or soft rag to apply the patina per manufacturer's instructions until all the solder is covered.

5. Wash your project again to remove any patina from the glass.

The finished piece is quite striking!

Fan Lamp Pattern

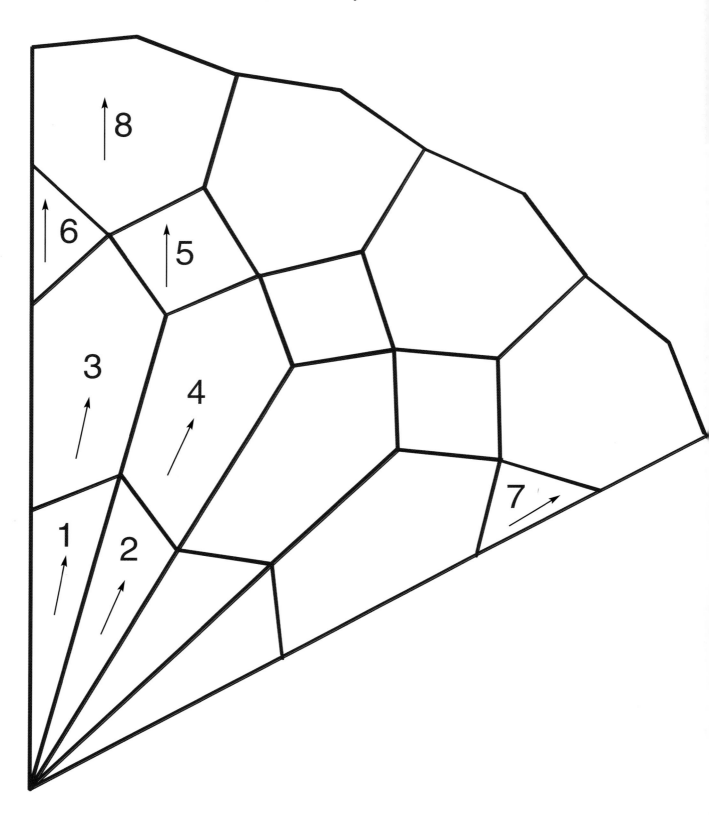

Small Tabletop Lamp (Project 3)

The moment you turn on your first lamp, you will be ready to start your next one. You will find yourself wanting to make a lamp for every room in the house. Your friends and family will be asking you where you got that beautiful lamp. You will beam with pride in knowing you have completed a piece of such great admiration and a piece of relative simplicity, since all you had to do was cut out three simple pieces, 12 times each.

For this project, you will need a gooseneck-type lamp base. I have found that such bases come in two different sizes and several different designs. They are readily found at stained glass stores or on the Internet (see Resources, page 124), along with the lamp rings.

As with previous projects in this book, you can plan on a square-foot of glass for each color you pick out. This lamp looks great even if you select the same color for all the patterns. You could easily make this lamp using 1 square-foot of glass!

Materials

- 1-square-foot caramel glass
- 1-square-foot wispy turquoise glass
- 15½" gooseneck-type lamp base
- 9"-high polystyrene form (3¾"-diameter base)
- 1 sheet each tracing paper, carbon paper, and plain white paper
- 1 roll ⁷⁄₃₂"-wide x 1.25mm-thick copper foil
- Several stick pins or small nails
- 2 to 4 thin wood strips
- Flux and flux brush
- 1 lb. 50/50 solder
- 8-oz. bottle patina and cloth
- Water and water bottle (for grinding)
- Hot water, brush, laundry soap, and bucket (for cleaning)
- Glasscutter
- Grinder
- Soldering iron
- Pliers
- Rubber gloves
- Scissors
- Pencil
- Pattern (page 116)

I have used two complementary colors for this lamp.

Preparing the Paper Pattern

1. Looking at the pattern on page 116, notice that each piece is numbered and the direction of grain noted.

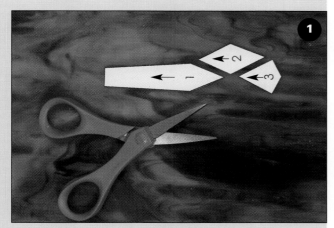

Notice the arrows on each pattern and how they depict the direction you want the grain in the glass to go.

2. Trace the pattern pieces onto paper.

3. After tracing the patterns onto paper, use your scissors to cut them out. These paper patterns will serve as the templates for cutting your glass.

Cutting the Pieces

1. Begin by first realizing how many pieces of each pattern piece you will need cut from the glass. Here is the number of pieces needed:
   - 12 of #1 from wispy turquoise
   - 12 of #2 from caramel
   - 12 of #3 from wispy turquoise

2. Beginning with the largest pattern piece (#1), reduce your glass to the size of the pattern and line it up on one end of the glass.

3. Using your ruler and paper pattern #1 as your guide, draw your line, as shown.

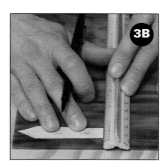
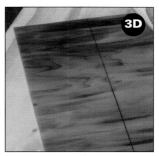

4. Score the glass directly on top of the line you just drew with your marking pen and separate the two pieces.

With a steady even pace, follow the line from one edge to the other.

5. Line up your pattern as shown in the photo here. Notice how the pattern doesn't line up flush to the edge of glass. Starting with the first piece in this position helps to align subsequent pieces and it also saves one additional score line.

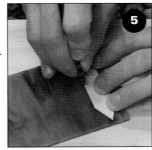

6. Score out your pattern.

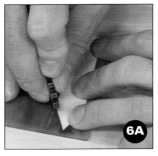

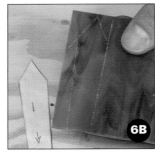

In photo 6A, notice how your first score line continues all the way to the edge of the glass, even though the pattern doesn't. Photo 6B shows the completely scored pattern.

7. Use your hands to separate the piece from the rest of the glass. With larger pieces, like this one, you should be able to easily snap it off.

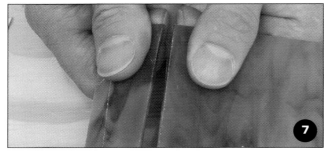

Get a good grip on both sides of the score line and snap in a downward motion.

8. Place #1 paper pattern in the reversed direction on the last score line as your edge, lining up the pattern flush to the edge of glass.

9. Flip the pattern every other piece until you have the desired number of #1 pieces.

10. Cut out pattern piece #3 by first lining up the paper pattern at the edge of the glass, as shown below.

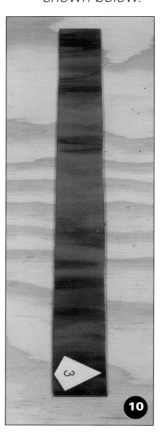

11. Score around the entire pattern.

12. Line the pattern up to the first one you scored, as shown.

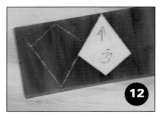

13. Using your hands, snap the piece from one end.

14. Position your cutter so the teeth are as close to the score line as possible. With a downward snap, remove the scrap.

15. Or, using your pliers, line up the jaws to the score line and close them up once they are in place.

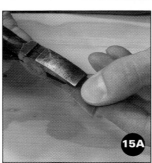

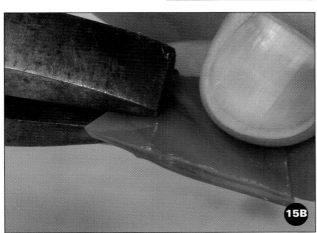

16. Snap quickly downward to remove scrap.

17. Score and cut pattern #2 as you did with #1 and #3.

Removing Scrap

1. Match up one of your glasscutter's teeth so it fits tightly on the glass piece.

2. Give the cutter a quick snap in a downward motion to remove the scrap.

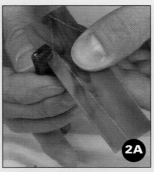

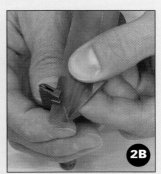

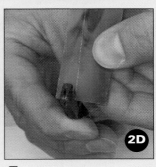

This is where I would position the cutter to remove this last piece.

Tip: You can also use your pliers to remove scrap, as shown below.

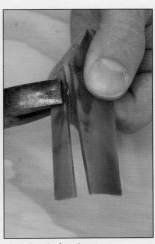

Line up the pliers as shown in the left photo to remove this piece, follow with a quick downward snap, and you are left with two pieces!

Grinding the Pieces

1. When all pieces are cut, clear the work area and line up the pieces at an accessible distance from the grinder.

Clear all scrap safely away with your brush.

Pieces stacked and ready next to grinder.

2. Set up the grinder with water in the reservoir.

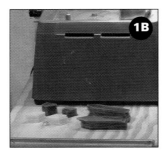

3. Using both hands, firmly hold one of the cut glass pattern pieces and slowly approach the grinding wheel at about a 10-degree angle to grind off the jagged bottom edge only. If necessary, refer to the photo for step 1 on page 50 in the *Why Grind?* section.

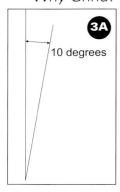

10 degrees

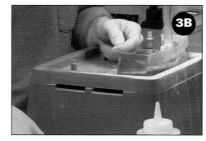

Don't forget the proper angle while grinding.

4. Gently touching the piece to the grinding wheel, apply light pressure against the grinder. If you contact the grinder too quickly, the wheel could grab the glass, tossing it out of your hands. This step is illustrated in the step 2 photo on page 50 in the *Why Grind?* section.

5. Carefully guide the piece around all the edges while grinding off just enough glass. Try to keep a slightly more than 90-degree angle with your piece. By maintaining this angle, your pieces will have a better chance of fitting together properly. Again, if a visual is needed here, this step is illustrated in the step 3 photo on page 50 in the *Why Grind?* section.

6. After grinding, examine the piece, making sure you have gotten all the sharp edges.

7. Repeat steps 3 through 6 for all pieces.

8. After grinding, wipe all pieces thoroughly.

9. When clean and dry, lay out the glass pieces in the design of your completed pattern on your workbench. If they line up properly on the workbench, they will line up on the form.

10. Check your pieces for any gaps between them. By closely examining them, you should be able to spot which piece(s) might be off. If you find any pieces that do not line up, now is the time to grind to make them fit better. Always grind a little at a time, and then check what you have done. Over-grinding can also cause pieces to fit improperly.

Ready to foil.

Foiling the Pieces

1. Begin with centering one glass piece on the sticky side of copper foil tape. Remember to start by peeling away a small section of tape from its backing (about 2").

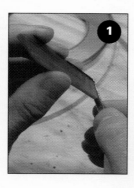

2. Keep your foil as even as possible on both sides. Lightly crimp the tape to the glass as you go.

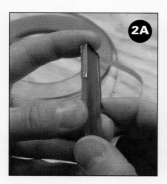
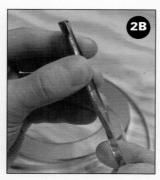

3. Once you have foiled around the piece, overlap the beginning foil edge by about 1/8" and tear from the roll with your fingers.

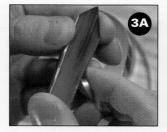
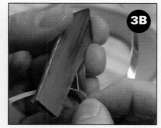

4. Using the back of your thumbnail, flatten both sides of your foil down to complete the process.

Completed first piece.

5. Repeat steps 1 through 4 for all remaining project pieces.

Don't be intimidated by the small pieces, they're not that difficult.

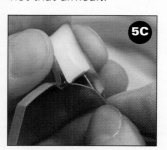

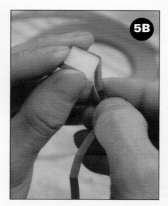
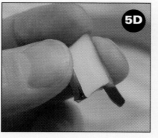

If you look closely, you will see how much to overlap the tape.

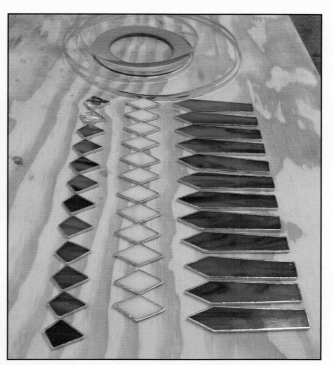

After foiling, line up your pieces in preparation for placing them on the form.

Using the Form

1. Start with a taped form, ready for your pieces to be placed on. Refer to page 76 for assistance with preparing your form, if necessary.

Form already taped.

2. Place your first piece on the form and line it up. It doesn't have to be perfect at this time. You will be making adjustments as you add to it.

3. Place two pins on the bottom, one at the top, and one along the left if you are going to add your pieces from left to right. Otherwise, place a pin on the right and add them to the left.

Slant your pins to help hold the glass in place.

4. Continue to add the first row of pieces, as shown, pinning them in place as you go.

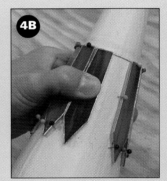

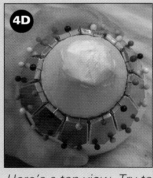

Here's a top view. Try to space the pieces with equal space between them.

Tip: As you can see by my example, the pieces don't fit perfectly tight. When starting out, don't worry as to how tight you get them to fit. This will come with experience and practice. The more lamps you make the easier it will be to fit your pieces together.

Soldering the Pieces

1. Plug in your solder iron and set up your fan so it is positioned to move fumes away from you.

First row ready to be soldered.

2. Start by fluxing your first row.

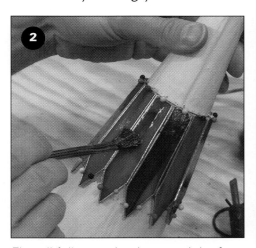

Flux all foil, completely around the form.

3. Unwind some solder from the roll and prop it up a little. You are going to need both hands: one for the iron and the other to hold the form.

4. When your iron gets hot enough, touch the tip of the solder and melt a little on your iron. Quickly apply it to the foil. Put a spot of solder on the top and bottom of each joint to hold it in place.

Spot soldering to hold your pieces in place.

5. When you have completely made it around the form, remove the pins from the bottom. You need to do this to add the second row of pieces.

Remove all the bottom pins.

6. Now add the second row, piece-by-piece and spot solder them in place as you go. Be very careful not to burn yourself. If you move quickly, the pieces will not become hot.

7. After getting the first two rows properly in place, go ahead and add more solder to the joints.

8. Add the third and final row, following the same directions as outlined for the other two rows.

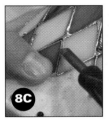
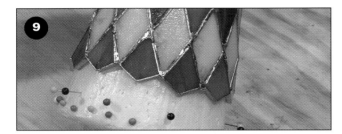

9. Remove the rest of the pins.

10. With all pins removed and all joints rough-soldered, lift the shade off the form, as shown below.

Carefully remove the shade from the form. Be sure not to squeeze too hard. Without the inside of the lamp soldered, the shade is still not very sturdy.

11. To help make the form more solid, you need to add solder to the top and bottom edges of the lamp, so start by adding flux to the edges.

12. Solder the edges, moving quickly around the rim.

Cover the entire rim with solder.

Before ...   and after.

13. Turn the lamp over and do the same to the bottom rim as in steps 11 and 12.

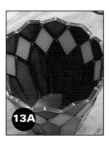

Tinning the Lamp Ring

1. Set the lampshade aside and get your lamp ring. It's time to tin the inside of it. You will need your pliers to hold onto the ring. It is going to get very hot!

2. While your iron is heating up, add flux to the ring, as shown below.

Add flux to the entire inside of the ring.

Safety Check: *Remember to turn your fan on before fluxing. With all the flux you put on, there will be a lot of smoke.*

3. Add a little solder to the tip of the iron and touch it to the ring. Work slowly in a circular motion in one area of the ring until it heats up.

4. Once the solder starts to plate the ring, continue to move slowly around the ring. When your soldering gets close to the pliers, put the ring down on the workbench and relocate your hold on the ring. Then continue where you left off.

Attaching the Lamp Ring

1. Place the tinned ring upside-down on the workbench.

2. Center your lampshade on top of the ring.

3. Add flux.

4. Spot solder ring in place in at least three spots around the perimeter. Be careful not to move it off-center while soldering.

5. Once spot soldered, add more solder to fill in the gaps.

Enough solder to hold it in place.

6. Holding onto the ring from the opposite side, position it so the solder flows into the gap while you rotate the shade.

Soldering the Inside

1. Elevate your lampshade by using two strips of wood as wedges, as shown, to keep the lamp from moving while you solder. It helps to have both hands free when soldering the inside.

2. Apply flux to the inside.

3. Add enough solder to fill all the joints.

Inside soldering completed.

4. Check it over completely when you're done.

Tip: The inside does not have to reflect the nice well-rounded even lines of solder like the outside, but make sure you don't leave any sharp points of solder behind. Such points present problems when cleaning or when adding the finish.

Tip: Try not to stay in one place too long. The soldering has a better chance of melting through without the support of the form, as shown in the accompanying photo. This is not uncommon and can be corrected when you finish solder on the outside. If it does melt through, leave the area and come back to fill it in when it cools down. The solder will continue to melt through if it doesn't cool down enough.

Solder melted through to the other side.

Carefully removing the glob of solder.

Soldering the Outside

Tip: *When finishing the outside, I like to use a cloth to hold onto the lamp. This way, I have more control as to where my solder flows. The cloth will allow you to hold on, since the shade is going to get very hot.*

1. *Flux the outside.*

2. *Even out the joints, adding solder where it's needed. Move at a steady pace for best results.*

Outside soldered, notice the nice even lines of solder.

3. *When the outside is completed, inspect the inside again, and make sure no solder has melted through. Check for any sharp areas of solder.*

4. *Wipe off as much flux as possible.*

Cloth bunched, allowing you to hold onto the lamp while soldering.

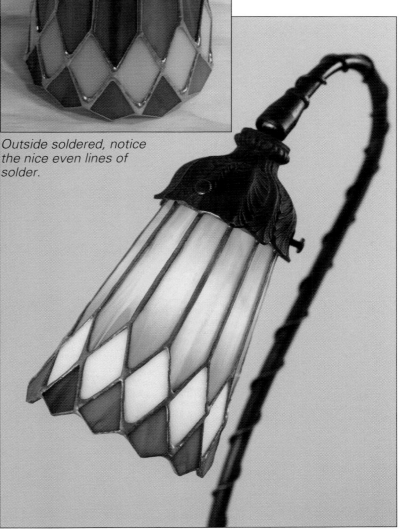

Finishing Your Lamp

1. *Fill a bucket with hot water and an ample amount of grease-fighting laundry soap.*

2. *Using a small scrub brush, thoroughly clean both sides of the entire piece. Make sure you get all of the residue off, as it is imperative you get the piece very clean.*

3. *Wipe your project dry.*

4. *Wearing rubber gloves, use a brush or soft rag to apply the patina, per the manufacturer's instructions, until all the solder is covered.*

5. *Wash your project again to remove any patina from the glass.*

Small Tabletop Lamp Pattern

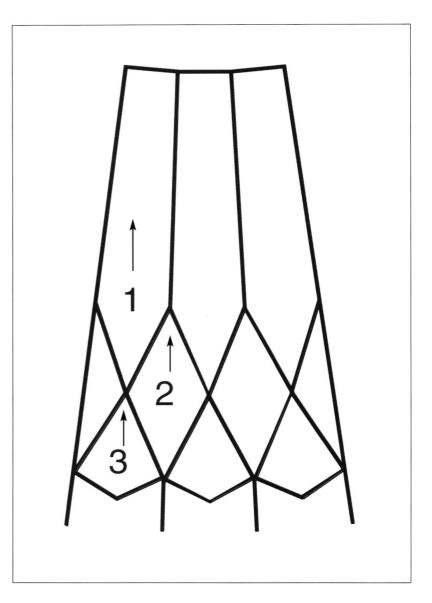

I have found lamp designing a little more challenging than working with flat panel designs, so I have included a few more lamp patterns. These lamp designs are more difficult, and include some pattern pieces with inside curves and smaller pieces.

Do you feel artistic and want to create your own lamp design? You will find the same basic pattern that I start with, when designing my lamps.

Use this pattern to design your own lampshade. For the smaller gooseneck lamp bases (15" high), design a shade about 3⅜" long. With taller goosenecks (19" high), stay around 4" long. These dimensions work the best.

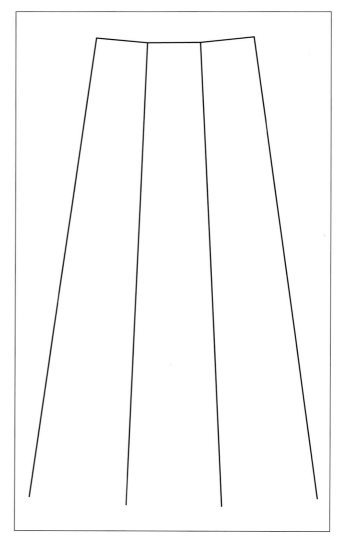

Lamp Base Design

Lamp Option 1

If you like shades of blue and green, this lamp is incredible. It consists of five patterns repeated 12 times each. The gooseneck lamp base is 19" high with a 4"-high lampshade. The design has a total of 60 pieces.

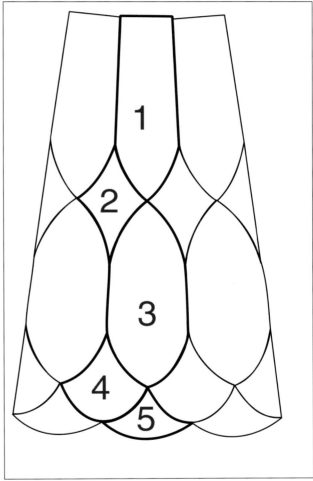

Lamp Pattern Option 1

Lamp Option 2

I get more compliments on this small lampshade. The one shown here is kept on my bedside table. Since I'm partial to shades of red, I chose a combination of red and orange for this shade with a 15" gooseneck base. The design is made up of four patterns repeated 12 times each. This shade is only 3⅜" high.

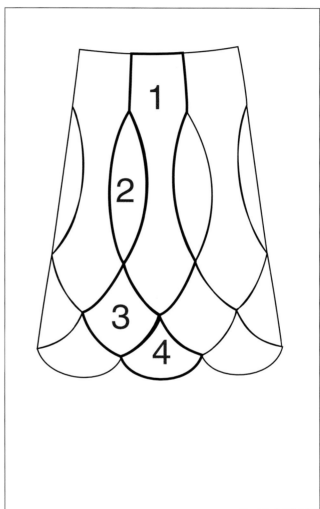

Lamp Pattern Option 2

Lamp Option 3

This design consists of four patterns repeated 12 times each.
I chose shades of orange, green, and gold on this particular design.
The shade has a total of 48 pieces with a height of 4" and is mounted
on a 19" base.

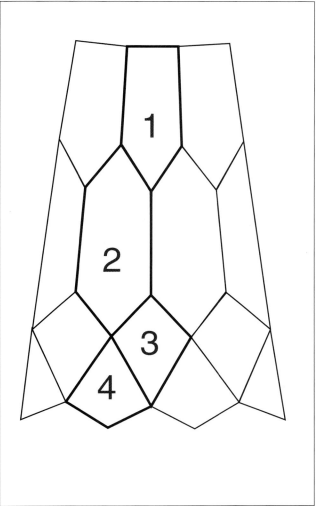

Lamp Pattern Option 3

Resources

D&L Stained Glass Supply, Inc.
4939 N. Broadway
Boulder, CO 80304
Phone: (800) 525-0940 or (303) 449-8737
Fax: (303) 442-3429
www.dlstainedglass.com
info@dlstainedglass.com
General supplies and
15½" Classic Gooseneck lamp base.

Delphi Stained Glass
3380 E. Jolly Road
Lansing, MI 48910
Phone: (800) 248-2048 or (517) 394-4631
Fax: (800) 748-0374 or (517) 394-5364
www.delphiglass.com
General supplies and #8004 ABR Art Deco
Fan Lady lamp base.

Ed Hoy's International
27625 Diehl Road
Warrenville, IL 60555
Phone: (800) 323-5668
www.edhoy.com
General supplies.

Stained Glass Warehouse
2350 Hendersonville Road
Arden, NC 28704
Phone: (888) 616-8892
www.stainedglasswarehouse.com
General supplies.

Houston Glass Craft Supply
2002 Brittmoore Road
Houston, TX 77043
Phone: (800) 231-0148
www.glasscraft.net
General supplies.

Index

Index

About the Author

Dan Alfuth has been an artist for more than 30 years. He grew up in Stevens Point, Wisconsin. With his wife and two daughters, Dan currently resides in the small village of Scandinavia, Wisconsin, overlooking the south branch of the Little Wolf River.

About 30 years ago, a lifelong friend, Rick Bartkowiak convinced Dan to visit a friend of his. Taking him up on the invitation, Dan was introduced to Leroy Newby, who became his mentor in stained glass work. Leroy was truly a master of the art.

Dan and Rick learned to work with glass through observation. Their classroom was in the basement of Leroy's home where they worked night after night. With Leroy's inspiration and incredible creations, they were well on their way to learning the art of stained glass.

After all these years of learning, Dan felt the time was right to share his knowledge. He hopes you have enjoyed the book and welcomes you to visit his Web site at: www.prismglassstudio.com.

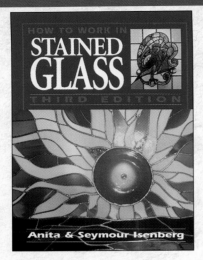

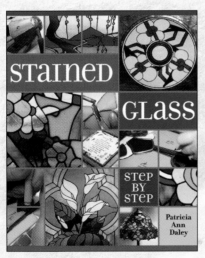